SCATTERGORIES

WORD SEARCH
PUZZLES

Mark Danna

**PUZZLE
WRIGHT
PRESS**

An imprint of Sterling
Publishing Co., Inc.

www.puzzlewright.com

Published by Sterling Publishing Co., Inc.
387 Park Avenue South, New York, NY 10016
© 2010 by Mark Danna
Distributed in Canada by Sterling Publishing
c/o Canadian Manda Group, 165 Dufferin Street
Toronto, Ontario, Canada M6K 3H6
Distributed in the United Kingdom by GMC Distribution Services
Castle Place, 166 High Street, Lewes, East Sussex, England BN7 1XU
Distributed in Australia by Capricorn Link (Australia) Pty. Ltd.
P.O. Box 704, Windsor, NSW 2756, Australia

Sterling ISBN 978-1-4027-5977-2

For information about custom editions, special sales, premium and
corporate purchases, please contact Sterling Special Sales
Department at 800-805-5489 or specialsales@sterlingpublishing.com.

CONTENTS

INTRODUCTION
4

PUZZLES
10

ANSWERS
130

WORD LISTS
150

INTRODUCTION

Scattergories Word Search Puzzles can be enjoyed in several ways. If you're a fan of Hasbro's classic Scattergories, this book gives you a way to play the game—and even compete!—when there's no one around to play with. If you simply love word searches, this book gives you a full 60 puzzles to solve, which you can do either with or without the word lists provided. And if you're the kind of person who likes to spice up your life with new and exciting combinations, this book will treat you to a rich and seamlessly intertwined game-and-puzzle experience!

SCATTERGORIES: THE BASIC GAME
Introduced in 1988, Scattergories is a party game in which players compete for points by naming unique items in various categories. Before play begins, each player gets a pad, pencil, and set of cards with lists. Pads contain sheets of paper divided into columns with 12 blank lines each for writing down answers. Each list has 12 different categories.

Before each round, players agree on which list is to be used, and one player rolls a 20-sided die to determine which letter of the alphabet will be the starting letter for every answer. One player then starts the timer, and everyone races to write down a word, name, or phrase to fit each category. When time is up, players compare answers. If you give the same answer as someone else, you score zero points for that category. If you give an answer that no one else has, you score one point. The player with the highest total after three rounds is the winner.

MODIFICATIONS
Our version is designed to be played by one person, and it is blended with word search puzzles, so we've made some modifications to the rules of the board game.

- Write down two answers, not just one, for every category.
- Score points for matching answers—ours!
- Find our answers as you solve word search puzzles—or simply skip to the answers in the back of the book.
- There are no rounds: Each Scattergories list and accompanying word search is a complete game in itself.

- There is no time limit unless you choose to self-impose one.
- Compete against yourself: Score as high as you can every game, and try to beat your best score or the score of your previous game.

BOOK LAYOUT

This book is laid out in two-page spreads. The left-hand page has a Scattergories list, starting letter, and blank lines for your category answers. The right-hand page has a word search grid that contains our category answers (plus bonus answers in the leftover letters) and a box for scoring.

ORDER OF PLAY

For order of play, we recommend that you fill in your answers to the categories; find our answers in the word search grid (or answer section); assign our answers to their correct categories; find additional answers in the grid's leftover letters; check the answers in the answer section; then determine your score.

TO START

Try to think of two answers that begin with the starting letter for every category on your list, and write them in their appropriate blanks. Answers can be words, names, or phrases. There are 24 answers—two for each of the 12 categories—for every game. (Detailed rules come later.)

THE WORD SEARCH

The goal in a word search puzzle is to find words hidden in a grid. A standard word search includes two main parts: a word list that tells you what words, names, and phrases are hidden in the grid; and the grid, which looks at first glance like a meaningless jumble of letters. Hidden words may run horizontally, vertically, or diagonally, but always in a straight line. Horizontal words go across forward or backward; vertical words go straight down or up; diagonal words slant from left-to-right or right-to-left and either upward or downward along an angle.

In this book, as part of the game, there's no word list next to the grid. It's up to you to uncover our 24 hidden answers that you're looking to match. (See "Scoring.") Again, there are two answers for each of the 12 categories.

As you find hidden words, you can loop them, draw a line through them, or circle each individual letter. Neatness counts ... because after you've found all the items in a grid, read the leftover letters from left to right, top to bottom, to spell out two or more additional answers for one of the categories. These extra answers may be worth bonus points. (See "Scoring.")

Since all answers in a grid begin with the same letter, solving should not be as daunting as you might think at first. However, if you find the search too hard or would rather skip it, you can turn to the answer section for our answers/word lists.

ASSIGNING ANSWERS TO CATEGORIES

As you find each answer in the word search grid, try to figure out which category it belongs to and write it in on the appropriate line next to one of your answers. In some cases, an answer may fit two different categories, so placing it in the correct category can be tricky. For example, ROOSEVELT could fit in the category "U.S. Presidents" or in "Famous Women" (if we're referring to Eleanor). However, there is only one way that all 24 of our answers in a game can be placed to fill each category with exactly two correct answers, so keep that in mind as you sort.

SCORING

Maximum score per game is 50 points. Scoring is as easy as ABC.

A Score 1 point for each good answer you've written. You, of course, will be the judge of what's good. In the board game, other players can challenge your answers and vote them unacceptable. Here only your vote counts. If you've come up with two answers for each of the 12 categories on a list, you score 2 x 12, or 24 points.

B Score 1 additional point for each one of your answers that matches one of ours for that category hidden in the grid. If you match an answer but it's in the wrong category, you don't score this point. Be sure to check your answers against those listed in the answer section when doing this scoring.

C Score 2 points for each answer of yours that matches an answer of ours that is spelled out in the leftover grid letters. These bonus answers will always come from exactly one category. You can find the category and bonus answers printed next to their appropriate answer grid in the answer section.

A scoring box appears below every word search puzzle grid. To get the maximum score of 50, you would need to get 24 points for your own written answers; 22 points for matching two answers each in the 11 categories not used in the leftover letters (2 x 11); and 4 points for having both of your answers in the 12th category match two of our answers spelled out in the leftover letters (2 x 2). (If you have answers in that category that match answers in the grid but not in the leftover letters, those answers are worth 1 point each, as for the other categories.)

Achieving a perfect score is like scoring a hole-in-one on every hole in a round of golf: it's darn near impossible. So try comparing yourself to this standard: Below 10 is poor; 10 to 20 is fair; 21 to 30 is good; 31 to 40 is excellent; 41 to 45 is phenomenal; 46 to 49 is awesome; 50 is utterly unbelievably amazing!

RULES FOR ACCEPTABLE ANSWERS

A The first (or only) word of your answer must begin with the given starting letter.

B The articles "A," "An," and "The" do not count for starting letters. Two examples: "S" is the starting letter for "The Shining" in the category "Movie Title"; T is the starting letter for "A Tale of Two Cities" in the category "Book." (Starting articles are omitted in our answers in the word search grids.)

C The exact same answer cannot be used twice in one list. Example: You cannot answer Daisy for "Flowers" and also for "Girls' Names."

D When answering with a proper name, you may use the first or last name as long as the starting letter is the first letter of your answer. Example: If the starting letter is "P" and the category is "Celebrity," your answer could be Paul Newman or Presley. If you use a last name for an answer, do not add a first name afterwards, as in Presley, Elvis (as you would do in the board game). Whenever our answer is just a last name, it will usually be for a person so famous that his or her last name can stand alone without there being any confusion as to who it is. Also, only that last name will appear in the word search grid. If the starting letter is used for the first name, the entire name will appear in the grid.

E For scoring purposes, if your answer is the singular version of a word and ours is the plural, or vice versa, count it as a match. The same thing applies to words with the same root. Example: PLAY and PLAYING would be a match.

F Do not score extra points for alliteration—where the same letter is repeated in an answer—as you can in the board game. Example: MARILYN MONROE is worth 1 point by itself, not 2.

SCORING AND SOLVING TIPS

Think of common answers. A big difference in scoring here versus the board game is that you want to match answers. In the spirit of good sportsmanship, we've chosen common answers as much as possible to give you a decent chance of matching us. So your strategy in this book, unlike in the board game, should be to come up with answers that are more, rather than less, obvious.

When solving a word search, be aware that no answer in a grid will ever be totally contained by another answer. For example, if the answers NEST and NESTLÉ appear in the same puzzle, look for NEST somewhere in the grid other than inside of NESTLÉ.

When determining answers in leftover letters, watch out for stray plural S's that may creep into—or be missing from—those leftovers, potentially causing confusion.

WORD LENGTHS

Each word search grid in this book is 11 x 15, so no answer will ever be longer than 15 letters. Answers are at least four letters long with few exceptions. When a three-letter answer does appear in a grid, it is indicated by an * after the name of the category.

WORD DIRECTIONS

In the hope that most readers will attempt to solve the word searches, we've tried to soften that challenge a bit by placing the majority of answer words horizontally or vertically (although often backward or upside-down). A much smaller percentage of words run diagonally.

FUN FACTS

There are 60 Scattergories games in this book. The 16 Scattergories lists included here are based on the ones packaged in the board game but have been modified as needed. Each list is used three or four times.

Feel free to jump around and play games in any order you like. The more difficult games tend to be those with a starting letter K or vowel.

The 20-sided die that comes with Hasbro's Scattergories game includes 20 different letters of the alphabet. Q, U, V, X, Y, and Z are excluded because each one is hard to use as a starting letter for all of the categories on any one list. Because it's tough to get two answers for K in every category, we've paired K once each with the U, V, and Y. When that happens, give one answer in every category using K and one using the other starting letter.

FINAL WORDS

If you know and love Scattergories, we hope you'll have a great time with this solitaire version of the game. If you've never played Scattergories, we hope you'll enjoy this version so much that you'll want to go out and find others to share the board game with. If you know and love word searches, we hope you'll like the hide-and-seek puzzles we've presented. And if you're never solved word searches, we hope you'll now discover their particular charm. So, welcome to *Scattergories Word Search Puzzles*. Let the games and puzzles begin!

SCATTERGORIES

Starting letter: T

1 Boys' Names
_____
_____

2 U.S. Cities
_____
_____

3 Things That Are Cold
_____
_____

4 School Supplies
_____
_____

5 Pro Sports Teams
_____
_____

6 Insects/Bugs
_____
_____

7 Breakfast Foods
_____
_____

8 Furniture
_____
_____

9 TV Shows
_____
_____

10 Things Found in the Ocean
_____
_____

11 Presidents
_____
_____

12 Product Names
_____
_____

Word List on page 150   Answer on page 130

```
T  C  S  E  L  C  A  T  N  E  T
E  I  E  R  T  W  O  O  A  I  E
X  N  V  E  L  D  I  A  G  P  L
T  A  L  L  A  H  A  S  S  E  E
B  T  O  Y  H  T  Z  T  A  F  T
O  I  W  T  O  N  T  R  I  X  U
O  T  R  I  S  C  U  I  T  S  B
K  T  E  R  R  Y  S  E  T  T  B
S  N  B  T  H  R  C  R  T  E  I
T  E  M  P  E  R  A  T  U  R  E
T  D  I  E  E  C  L  A  N  M  S
S  I  T  C  A  O  O  B  D  I  M
P  R  C  E  A  N  O  L  R  T  Y
T  T  T  K  A  X  S  E  A  E  I
T  I  T  A  N  S  A  M  O  H  T
```

SCORING

Your answers (1 pt. each) _____

Matching answers
in the grid (1 pt. each) _____

Matching answers
in the hidden message
(2 pts. each) _____

GRAND TOTAL _____

11

SCATTERGORIES

Starting letter: F

1 Famous Females

_____

_____

2 Medicine/Drugs

_____

_____

3 Things Made of Metal

_____

_____

4 Hobbies

_____

_____

5 People in Uniform

_____

_____

6 Things You Plug In

_____

_____

7 Animals

_____

_____

8 Languages

_____

_____

9 Names of People in the Bible

_____

_____

10 Junk Food

_____

_____

11 Things That Grow

_____

_____

12 Companies

_____

_____

Word List on page 151   Answer on page 130

```
H  F  R  I  D  A  K  A  H  L  O
C  I  F  R  F  A  R  S  I  F  U
N  R  F  E  L  I  X  R  F  R  E
E  S  I  T  O  F  S  E  I  I  C
R  T  F  I  W  U  E  K  L  E  N
F  L  U  M  E  D  I  C  I  N  E
L  I  R  N  R  G  R  O  N  D  F
O  E  S  E  G  E  F  L  G  S  O
N  U  F  H  H  R  L  T  C  H  O
A  T  O  A  I  T  E  O  A  I  T
S  E  R  E  N  N  A  O  B  P  B
E  N  D  E  R  S  G  F  I  S  A
F  A  X  M  A  C  H  I  N  E  L
N  N  A  M  E  R  I  F  E  N  L
A  T  E  R  R  E  F  I  T  L  S
```

SCATTERGORIES

Starting letter: S

1 Articles of Clothing
_____
_____

2 Desserts
_____
_____

3 Car Parts
_____
_____

4 Things Found on a Map
_____
_____

5 Athletes
_____
_____

6 4-Letter Words
_____
_____

7 Items in a Refrigerator
_____
_____

8 Farm Animals
_____
_____

9 Street Names
_____
_____

10 Things at the Beach
_____
_____

11 Colors
_____
_____

12 Tools
_____
_____

Word List on page 152   Answer on page 130

```
S  D  A  E  N  S  M  A  S  K  I
E  S  E  P  I  A  S  O  U  T  H
N  R  S  S  T  S  K  I  R  T  K
O  A  A  R  E  K  T  E  F  L  R
I  Y  S  E  B  A  P  E  E  H  S
S  A  M  V  R  T  T  V  R  W  P
N  A  R  I  E  C  O  B  I  A  K
E  S  N  R  H  H  S  N  E  C  O
P  H  C  D  S  E  E  C  O  L  H
S  C  S  W  C  W  E  L  S  S  T
U  A  O  E  R  A  B  P  I  O  N
S  N  C  R  R  N  S  L  N  D  E
S  I  K  C  U  B  V  T  K  A  V
L  P  S  S  A  E  I  Y  L  E  E
R  S  H  O  R  T  C  A  K  E  S
```

SCATTERGORIES

Starting letter: I

1 Heroes
_____
_____

2 Gifts/Presents
_____
_____

3 Words of Affection
_____
_____

4 Occupations
_____
_____

5 Chemical Elements
_____
_____

6 Vehicles
_____
_____

7 Tropical Locations
_____
_____

8 College Majors
_____
_____

9 Dairy Products
_____
_____

10 Male Singers ·
_____
_____

11 Items in Your Purse/Wallet
_____
_____

12 Mythological Characters
_____
_____

Word List on page 153   Answer on page 131

```
M A E R C E C I S S I
I M P A L A O I S E R
M R L N V D S N A L O
Y E O O I I I T I B T
O I I N D O N E S I A
U V E I C I D R E D R
R O S S A V Y I L E T
S R Y L R A C O G R S
K Y T E D N A R I C U
L I S G V H R D A N L
I B U P R O F E N I L
M T R O R E L S T I I
E N A I T A L I A N T
C E C R P R E G T E I
I R I S H L I N E N R
```

SCATTERGORIES

Starting letter: M

1 Sandwiches

_____

_____

2 Items in a Catalog

_____

_____

3 World Leaders/
Politicians

_____

_____

4 School Subjects

_____

_____

5 Excuses for Being Late

_____

_____

6 Ice Cream Flavors

_____

_____

7 Cosmetics

_____

_____

8 Television Stars

_____

_____

9 Things in a Park

_____

_____

10 Foreign Cities

_____

_____

11 Stones/Gems

_____

_____

12 Musical Instruments

_____

_____

Word List on page 154   Answer on page 131

```
F  A  O  L  T  A  E  M  O  S  S
M  O  L  L  A  H  S  R  A  M  N
M  U  S  I  C  T  I  M  E  I  R
I  E  R  E  A  L  D  M  E  S  M
T  N  I  L  O  D  N  A  M  S  O
T  O  M  I  G  R  A  I  N  E  N
E  T  L  M  O  C  H  A  B  D  T
N  S  M  A  L  A  C  H  I  T  E
S  N  S  A  C  A  R  A  M  H  C
O  O  P  C  O  N  E  U  R  E  R
C  O  E  U  A  N  M  E  M  B  I
R  M  I  L  E  Y  C  Y  R  U  S
A  M  I  N  T  K  A  N  I  S  T
M  M  O  U  N  T  A  I  N  L  O
A  A  R  A  C  S  A  M  A  T  H
```

SCATTERGORIES

Starting letter: O

1 Nicknames

7 Mammals

2 Things in the Sky

8 Historical Figures

3 Pizza Toppings

9 Things You Might Be Afraid Of

4 Colleges/Universities

10 Terms of Measurement*

5 Seafood

11 Items in a Living Room

6 Countries/Regions

12 Book Titles

Word List on page 155   Answer on page 131

```
Y  E  R  P  S  O  O  U  N  C  E
H  O  N  T  H  E  R  O  A  D  O
G  N  E  H  O  O  I  O  M  R  R
U  I  G  G  L  R  C  R  T  A  A
O  O  Y  I  O  A  O  E  E  A  N
R  N  X  R  N  L  H  G  L  D  G
E  O  O  W  O  S  I  A  T  O  U
G  Z  B  E  A  U  O  N  U  O  T
N  Z  E  L  I  R  S  O  O  U  A
A  Y  R  L  N  G  T  R  L  H  N
R  E  L  I  A  E  A  M  L  U  M
O  L  I  V  E  R  T  W  I  S  T
T  K  N  R  C  Y  E  U  E  A  L
F  A  R  O  O  P  E  N  S  E  A
I  O  C  T  O  P  U  S  E  N  D
```

SCATTERGORIES

Starting letter: D

1 Fictional Characters

_____

_____

2 Menu Items

_____

_____

3 Magazines

_____

_____

4 Capitals

_____

_____

5 Kinds of Candy

_____

_____

6 Items You Save Up to Buy

_____

_____

7 Footwear

_____

_____

8 Something You Keep Hidden

_____

_____

9 Items in a Suitcase

_____

_____

10 Things With Tails

_____

_____

11 Sports Equipment

_____

_____

12 Crimes

_____

_____

Word List on page 156   Answer on page 132

```
D  R  D  E  S  S  E  R  T  S  A
G  N  I  R  D  N  O  M  A  I  D
G  O  G  F  D  E  T  A  I  L  S
G  N  I  L  A  E  D  G  U  R  D
G  R  T  N  N  C  N  D  S  S  U
N  E  A  D  C  R  E  V  S  P  B
I  V  L  A  E  I  E  D  E  O  B
D  O  C  K  S  I  D  E  R  R  L
U  C  A  A  H  D  N  D  D  D  E
A  S  M  R  O  G  I  R  W  U  B
R  I  E  O  E  L  D  A  A  C  U
F  D  R  E  B  V  V  W  R  K  B
E  I  A  E  L  R  I  E  F  Y  B
D  A  R  K  S  E  C  R  E  T  L
A  T  D  I  S  C  U  S  D  Y  E
```

SCORING

Your answers (1 pt. each) _____

Matching answers
in the grid (1 pt. each) _____

Matching answers
in the hidden message
(2 pts. each) _____

GRAND TOTAL _____

SCATTERGORIES

Starting letter: G

1 Things That Are Sticky

_____

_____

2 Awards/Ceremonies

_____

_____

3 Cars

_____

_____

4 Spices/Herbs

_____

_____

5 Bad Habits

_____

_____

6 Cosmetics/Toiletries

_____

_____

7 Celebrities

_____

_____

8 Cooking Utensils

_____

_____

9 Reptiles/Amphibians

_____

_____

10 National Park Sights

_____

_____

11 Leisure Activities

_____

_____

12 Things That You're
Allergic To

_____

_____

Word List on page 157   Answer on page 132

```
R E S A E R G R A S S
E G G E O N N R E S G
S E R T E R A O U S A
Y G A S G U Z Z L E R
E G N I L B M A G R D
G I D L U M O R T P E
G R C O T R S E G C N
G R A T E R T T O I I
R Y N D N G R T M L N
E M Y A U E G E R G
M M O L G A E L E A O
L A N N R L T L C G L
I R I B G A X I K Y F
N G O O F I N G O F F
G E N E S I M M O N S
```

SCATTERGORIES

Starting letter: A

1 Restaurants
_____
_____

2 Notorious People
_____
_____

3 Fruits
_____
_____

4 Things in a Medicine
Cabinet
_____
_____

5 Toys
_____
_____

6 Household Chores
_____
_____

7 Bodies of Water
_____
_____

8 Authors
_____
_____

9 Halloween Costumes
_____
_____

10 Weapons
_____
_____

11 Things That Are Round
_____
_____

12 Words Associated
With Exercise
_____
_____

Word List on page 158   Answer on page 132

```
A N T A M A Z O N S O
M U C C A D V I L M I
N H C I N D A B Y R T
E E A B I A C A A A E
T H P O M I T P R R G
S T R R A R I P T R R
U A I E L T O L H A A
A L C A P O N E S N T
T I O R O T F P A G Y
L T T R M I I N R E R
A T B O A R G A B F E
N A R W I E U I Y I H
T T I N L S R S S L C
I E I B O R E A L E R
C L E R Y V O M I S A
```

SCORING

Your answers (1 pt. each)	_____
Matching answers in the grid (1 pt. each)	_____
Matching answers in the hidden message (2 pts. each)	_____
GRAND TOTAL	_____

SCATTERGORIES

Starting letter: N

1 Sports

_____

_____

2 Song Titles

_____

_____

3 Parts of the Body

_____

_____

4 Ethnic Foods

_____

_____

5 Things You Shout

_____

_____

6 Birds

_____

_____

7 Girls' Names

_____

_____

8 U.S. States

_____

_____

9 Items in the Kitchen

_____

_____

10 Villains/Monsters

_____

_____

11 Flowers

_____

_____

12 Chemical Elements

_____

_____

Word List on page 159   Answer on page 133

```
N A T N E W Y O R K I
R N E O N D A C L I M
E E N I N E P I N S O
V S N E I H X N A A A
E S O A G C T T S A N
N I R S H T S N T R O
O E T H T A U U U A S
W M H S I R S T R C T
H A D O N E S H T S R
E G A H G S I A I A I
R E K C A R C T U N L
E M O A L U R C M A N
M A T N E N A H N A O
A N A P K I N S A R A
N I T R O G E N E C K
```

SCATTERGORIES

Starting letter: B

1 Baby Foods
_____
_____

2 Famous Duos and Trios
_____
_____

3 Things Found in a Desk
_____
_____

4 Vacation Spots
_____
_____

5 Diseases
_____
_____

6 Words Associated
With Money
_____
_____

7 Items in a Vending
Machine
_____
_____

8 Movie Titles
_____
_____

9 Games
_____
_____

10 Things You Wear
_____
_____

11 Beers
_____
_____

12 Things at a Circus
_____
_____

Word List on page 150   Answer on page 133

```
B  B  A  B  Y  R  U  T  H  R  Y
A  L  B  U  D  W  E  I  S  E  R
D  U  A  R  E  L  A  D  N  D  E
U  E  T  B  E  E  T  S  O  I  N
M  S  M  C  B  I  N  G  O  R  O
R  B  A  H  A  M  A  S  L  K  I
E  R  N  B  A  T  R  G  L  C  T
B  O  T  U  L  I  S  M  A  A  A
I  T  A  E  L  G  G  O  B  B  T
G  H  B  I  B  O  T  T  L  E  S
B  E  R  I  B  E  R  I  B  R  F
U  R  N  I  B  A  N  A  N  A  O
C  S  L  B  E  N  N  H  E  B  X
K  L  B  E  C  K  S  F  U  I  O
S  E  E  G  E  E  B  T  S  R  B
```

SCATTERGORIES

Starting letter: W

1 Vegetables

_____

_____

2 States

_____

_____

3 Things You Throw Away

_____

_____

4 Occupations

_____

_____

5 Appliances

_____

_____

6 Cartoon Characters

_____

_____

7 Types of Drink

_____

_____

8 Musical Groups

_____

_____

9 Store/Business Names

_____

_____

10 Things at a Football Game

_____

_____

11 Trees

_____

_____

12 Personality Traits

_____

_____

Word List on page 151   Answer on page 133

```
W  I  L  E  E  C  O  Y  O  T  E
W  I  N  R  W  W  R  S  H  W  S
Y  I  R  E  R  A  F  L  E  W  S
W  W  E  H  W  L  L  T  S  U  E
A  D  V  S  A  N  N  D  U  T  R
S  S  I  A  H  U  Y  W  O  A  C
T  T  E  W  R  T  A  R  H  N  R
E  R  C  S  G  N  I  W  G  G  E
N  A  E  B  X  A  W  M  N  C  T
E  M  R  W  W  Y  A  W  I  L  A
D  L  E  Y  O  B  R  E  T  A  W
O  A  D  M  L  H  D  N  S  N  I
O  W  I  N  L  Y  E  D  E  W  I
W  N  W  T  I  H  N  Y  W  D  R
G  A  W  N  W  H  I  S  K  E  Y
```

SCATTERGORIES

Starting letter: P

1 Things at a Picnic
_____
_____

2 Things That Are Soft
_____
_____

3 Scary Movies
_____
_____

4 Things at the White House
_____
_____

5 Things That Kids Play With
_____
_____

6 Things at a Wedding
_____
_____

7 Hot Places
_____
_____

8 Things in Outer Space
_____
_____

9 Found in a Dorm
_____

10 Black and White Things
_____
_____

11 Famous Singers
_____
_____

12 Things at an Amusement Park
_____

Word List on page 152   Answer on page 134

```
P P R E S S C O R P S
P A L A T E P P R H P
R R P E N G U I N O L
I K I L R E Z Z A E U
E I L P A E Z Z S N T
S N L O S T L A L I O
T G O T E T E O Y X R
P L W A P A N V U L E
P O L T E R G E I S T
S T I O A M I N R O S
P R E S I D E N T A O
N P L A A R T O C N P
P U L L T O Y T T E P
P P P A R T Y A T B O
P R E D A T O R O N E
```

SCATTERGORIES

Starting letter: H

1 Worn Above the Waist
_____
_____

2 Things That Are Bright
_____
_____

3 Things That Have Numbers
_____
_____

4 Found in a Gym/Health Club
_____
_____

5 Things on a Safari
_____
_____

6 Ways to Say Hi and Bye
_____
_____

7 Things From the Sixties
_____
_____

8 Holiday Things
_____
_____

9 Items in an Office
_____
_____

10 Things in Pairs or Sets
_____
_____

11 Things on an Interstate
_____
_____

12 Things in Las Vegas
_____

Word List on page 153   Answer on page 134

```
H A H E L M E T A H H
I X I R D N E H T C E
R N G E T O I I S N A
H H H O L P O G I U D
A H H L P M B H V P O
N N E I U R G W A E N
U H E A H H E A L L C
K S L Y D O A Y A O O
K S S D H L P S T H L
A H O T E L I H S H L
H A T H A Y O G A U I
G R O H E M A N H N S
E R N H O N D A E T I
L A H O U S E S S E O
T H P P R I N T E R N
```

SCATTeRGORIeS

Starting letter: E

1 Things at a Zoo

_____

_____

2 Things With Motors

_____

_____

3 Things That Fly

_____

_____

4 Found at a Salad Bar

_____

_____

5 Words Ending in "LY"

_____

_____

6 Things on a Hiking Trip

_____

_____

7 Mythological Characters

_____

_____

8 Annual Celebrations

_____

_____

9 Found in a Classroom

_____

_____

10 Party Things

_____

_____

11 Reasons to Skip School/Work

_____

_____

12 Titles People Have

_____

_____

Word List on page 154   Answer on page 134

```
E  E  T  N  A  H  P  E  L  E  E
L  A  E  V  I  D  E  N  T  L  Y
G  S  R  D  E  R  A  T  O  O  R
A  T  U  T  C  C  A  T  S  R  A
E  E  M  P  H  Y  S  E  M  A  B
X  R  O  A  O  D  I  R  E  C  Y
C  U  A  S  X  T  A  S  A  S  G
I  S  Y  S  P  E  E  Y  Q  E  R
T  O  U  M  E  A  R  A  C  H  E
E  L  E  C  T  R  I  C  F  A  N
M  C  A  T  I  L  O  N  E  T  E
E  N  V  I  R  O  N  M  E  N  T
N  E  M  P  E  R  O  R  N  G  L
T  N  A  L  P  G  G  E  I  S  H
Y  L  I  S  A  E  N  G  I  N  E
```

SCATTERGORIES

Starting letter: C

1 Things in a Desert

_____

_____

2 Things in a Mystery Novel

_____

_____

3 Computer Lingo

_____

_____

4 Loud Things

_____

_____

5 Kinds of Soups/Stews

_____

_____

6 Math Terms

_____

_____

7 Underground Things

_____

_____

8 Things in the Wild West

_____

_____

9 Things in an Airport

_____

_____

10 Words with Double Letters

_____

_____

11 Found in New York City

_____

_____

12 Things Seen in a Castle

_____

_____

Word List on page 155   Answer on page 135

```
E  L  B  I  T  A  P  M  O  C  C
N  O  D  C  H  O  W  D  E  R  Y
A  A  E  C  A  M  E  L  C  C  R
J  M  N  O  O  C  O  C  A  D  L
Y  M  R  N  C  S  T  O  M  R  A
I  C  C  I  A  U  C  N  B  T  A
M  L  R  G  T  L  C  M  E  S  C
A  A  I  U  O  U  O  C  L  E  H
L  T  M  R  F  C  P  L  L  J  E
A  T  I  A  A  L  I  A  S  T  C
C  E  N  T  R  A  L  P  A  R  K
L  R  A  I  M  C  O  A  O  U  I
U  C  L  O  S  M  T  M  O  O  N
E  A  N  N  S  D  W  O  R  C  D
```

SCATTERGORIES

Starting letter: W

1 Boys' Names
_____
_____

2 U.S. Cities
_____
_____

3 Things That Are Cold
_____
_____

4 School Supplies
_____
_____

5 Pro Sports Teams
_____
_____

6 Insects
_____
_____

7 Breakfast Foods
_____
_____

8 Furniture
_____
_____

9 TV Shows
_____
_____

10 Things Found in the Ocean
_____
_____

11 Presidents
_____
_____

12 Things in a Courtroom
_____
_____

Word List on page 156   Answer on page 135

```
T  U  O  E  T  I  W  P  S  A  W
I  W  W  S  D  R  A  Z  I  W  A
R  A  R  E  T  N  I  W  W  H  L
W  I  C  K  E  R  C  H  A  I  R
A  L  E  L  A  V  W  A  Y  T  U
C  W  N  L  W  L  I  L  N  E  S
O  A  O  W  A  E  A  L  E  S  W
A  F  T  E  E  H  S  K  R  O  W
N  F  G  U  K  S  W  L  E  X  G
O  L  N  A  W  I  T  N  E  S  S
S  E  I  T  A  E  H  W  N  Y  W
L  H  H  E  W  I  C  H  I  T  A
I  E  S  L  W  A  L  T  O  N  S
W  W  A  L  L  U  N  I  T  I  G
N  G  W  I  N  D  S  T  O  R  M
```

SCATTERGORIES

Starting letter: M

1 Famous Females
_____
_____

2 Medicine/Drugs
_____
_____

3 Things Made of Metal
_____
_____

4 Hobbies
_____
_____

5 People in Uniform
_____
_____

6 Things You Plug In
_____
_____

7 Animals
_____
_____

8 Languages
_____
_____

9 Names of People in the Bible
_____
_____

10 Junk Food
_____
_____

11 Flowers
_____
_____

12 Companies
_____
_____

Word List on page 157   Answer on page 135

```
X M M M A C R A M E O
O T F O S O R C I M M
L N O N D M S E D M O
A I U G S E O K S O T
A R E O X M M V H M O
M A I L C A R R I E R
A D R I O N K X P E E
G N U A Y Y E M M O S
N A C N N R G M A M D
O M E T H A D O N E U
L O I O A M E B N T D
I S R E C M L I O L K
A M A R I G O L D I L
I N M & M S M E A F I
K K C I D Y B O M E M
```

SCATTERGORIES

Starting letter: J

1 Articles of Clothing
_____
_____

2 Candy
_____
_____

3 Games
_____
_____

4 Countries
_____
_____

5 Athletes
_____
_____

6 Comic Book
Characters
_____
_____

7 Items in a Refrigerator
_____
_____

8 Animals
_____
_____

9 Presidents
_____
_____

10 Vehicles
_____
_____

11 Colors
_____
_____

12 Tools
_____
_____

Word List on page 158　　　　　　Answer on page 136

R	E	K	A	E	R	B	W	A	J	J
A	S	C	K	R	E	T	A	J	J	E
I	K	S	T	E	J	Y	S	E	R	S
E	C	Y	J	W	J	L	G	F	O	J
J	A	W	S	O	F	L	I	F	E	D
A	J	D	R	R	J	E	J	E	B	D
P	H	D	J	H	U	J	P	R	U	E
A	A	P	A	T	G	U	J	S	J	R
N	R	S	S	N	H	J	U	O	U	D
J	A	M	M	I	E	S	I	N	J	E
S	G	O	I	L	A	K	C	A	J	G
Y	N	G	N	E	D	B	E	A	R	D
A	E	A	E	V	J	U	D	M	P	U
S	J	O	E	A	R	E	G	G	O	J
U	I	T	J	J	O	H	N	S	O	N

SCATTERGORIES

Starting letter: K & Y

1 Drinks

2 Holidays

3 Toys

4 Monsters

5 Baking Needs

6 Vehicles

7 Tropical Locations

8 Games

9 Dairy Products

10 Things in a Souvenir Shop

11 Insects

12 Languages

Word List on page 159   Answer on page 136

```
Y  K  N  O  Y  I  D  D  I  S  H
U  Y  R  I  F  E  K  I  C  K  N
G  A  K  A  B  O  A  D  A  E  A
O  N  A  T  A  C  U  Y  U  Y  E
T  K  O  E  K  E  A  T  A  C  R
R  E  T  K  C  K  I  A  H  H  O
U  E  Y  C  G  T  Z  K  A  A  K
P  S  W  A  L  N  R  Y  E  I  A
P  C  A  J  A  C  I  U  H  N  R
I  A  T  W  Y  A  M  K  G  A  O
K  P  K  O  O  L  A  I  D  O  S
M  I  H  L  E  E  Z  T  H  A  Y
O  A  T  L  M  O  T  O  O  R  R
Y  I  T  E  Y  Y  O  Y  O  C  U
Y  C  L  Y  E  Y  E  A  S  T  P
```

SCORING

Your answers (1 pt. each) _____

Matching answers
in the grid (1 pt. each) _____

Matching answers
in the hidden message
(2 pts. each) _____

GRAND TOTAL _____

SCATTERGORIES

Starting letter: R

1 Sandwiches
_____
_____

2 Things in a Catalog
_____
_____

3 World Leaders/
Politicians
_____
_____

4 School Subjects
_____
_____

5 Excuses for Being Late
_____
_____

6 Ice Cream Flavors
_____
_____

7 Things That
Jump/Bounce
_____
_____

8 Television Stars
_____
_____

9 Things in a Park
_____
_____

10 Foreign Cities*
_____
_____

11 Stones/Gems
_____
_____

12 Musical Instruments
_____
_____

Word List on page 150   Answer on page 136

```
S  D  A  O  R  Y  K  C  O  R  E
G  F  C  O  U  A  R  R  A  B  R
U  E  M  E  B  R  A  E  R  G  U
R  E  P  U  B  L  I  C  A  N  S
O  B  N  T  E  E  R  O  N  I  O
S  T  O  R  R  A  R  R  O  D  L
E  S  I  A  B  H  U  D  U  A  C
T  A  G  B  A  C  M  E  T  L  D
T  O  I  B  L  A  R  R  O  B  A
A  R  L  I  L  R  A  E  F  R  O
S  M  E  T  I  L  I  A  T  E  R
T  I  R  U  Y  A  S  G  I  L  A
O  D  R  U  B  Y  I  A  M  L  V
N  I  B  O  R  E  N  N  E  O  E
E  R  E  A  D  I  N  G  H  R  N
```

SCATTERGORIES

Starting letter: S

1 Nicknames

_____

_____

2 Things in the Sky

_____

_____

3 Pizza Toppings

_____

_____

4 Colleges/Universities

_____

_____

5 Fish

_____

_____

6 Countries

_____

_____

7 Things That Have Spots

_____

_____

8 Historical Figures

_____

_____

9 Things You Might Be Afraid Of

_____

_____

10 Terms of Measurement

_____

_____

11 Furniture

_____

_____

12 Book Titles

_____

_____

Word List on page 151   Answer on page 137

```
S  H  A  K  E  S  P  E  A  R  E
O  T  K  S  D  Q  A  H  S  E  A
F  I  N  S  U  U  T  U  U  T  S
A  M  A  H  T  A  S  S  C  T  T
R  S  L  E  I  R  A  T  N  E  A
E  T  I  L  L  E  T  A  S  L  N
S  A  R  V  O  M  C  N  U  T  F
P  L  S  E  S  I  H  D  E  E  O
R  I  M  S  A  L  M  N  S  L  R
S  N  O  W  L  E  O  P  A  R  D
A  I  B  A  R  A  I  D  U  A  S
L  K  S  D  N  O  C  E  S  C  T
M  S  S  E  N  I  D  R  A  S  A
O  N  O  W  F  L  A  K  G  E  R
N  S  S  T  R  A  N  G  E  R  S
```

SCATTERGORIES

Starting letter: L

1 Fictional Characters
_____
_____

2 Menu Items
_____
_____

3 Magazines
_____
_____

4 Capitals
_____
_____

5 Kinds of Candy
_____
_____

6 Items You Save Up to Buy
_____
_____

7 Sold in a Shoe Store
_____
_____

8 Something You Keep Hidden
_____
_____

9 Items in a Suitcase
_____
_____

10 Things With Tails
_____
_____

11 Sports Equipment
_____
_____

12 Crimes
_____
_____

Word List on page 152   Answer on page 137

```
L O L L I P O P L L L
S L A O O N G R A O L
P J P O E N E N N O A
O S T H I T G D S T C
R E O N S A O I I I R
D C P B S N S K N N O
N A O A A I O L G G S
O L L V L O A F E R S
M E A R L L I L I F E
E S R N O I L T R T S
L U C Y V A N P E L T
L X E E E E M I G E I
R E N M R A G I N D C
L L Y E G O L U I G K
B M A L F O G E L A S
```

SCATTERGORIES

Starting letter: P

1 Things That Are Sticky

2 Awards/Ceremonies

3 Cars

4 Spices/Herbs

5 Composers

6 Cosmetics/Toiletries

7 Celebrities

8 Cooking Utensils

9 Reptiles/Amphibians

10 Buildings

11 Leisure Activities

12 Things That You're Allergic To

Word List on page 153   Answer on page 137

```
P  P  A  P  Y  C  E  T  S  A  P
H  U  E  L  E  O  I  B  E  P  E
P  L  L  P  L  T  L  O  P  A  A
A  I  R  P  S  P  S  O  A  M  B
I  T  T  O  R  A  V  A  P  E  O
N  Z  P  L  A  L  T  E  R  L  D
T  E  P  L  P  A  H  E  I  A  Y
E  R  R  E  R  C  P  U  K  A  R
D  E  O  N  S  E  C  P  A  N  S
T  K  K  R  R  P  A  G  O  D  A
U  O  O  E  E  E  L  L  P  E  O
R  P  F  L  D  U  L  L  E  R  P
T  L  I  E  W  P  R  I  U  S  E
L  N  E  E  O  P  Y  T  H  O  N
E  C  V  P  P  U  C  C  I  N  I
```

SCATTERGORIES

Starting letter: B

1 Restaurants

_____

_____

2 Notorious People

_____

_____

3 Fruits

_____

_____

4 Things in a Medicine Cabinet

_____

_____

5 Toys

_____

_____

6 Household Activities

_____

_____

7 Bodies of Water

_____

_____

8 Authors

_____

_____

9 Halloween Costumes

_____

_____

10 Weapons

_____

_____

11 Things That Are Round

_____

_____

12 Words Associated With Exercise

_____

_____

Word List on page 154   Answer on page 138

S	P	E	C	I	B	U	C	K	B	B
A	N	B	Y	D	A	N	F	L	A	U
A	O	B	A	L	T	I	C	L	C	M
E	T	E	I	O	M	R	L	E	G	B
N	T	I	G	N	A	E	E	B	N	L
B	U	B	R	R	N	F	L	R	I	E
O	B	R	O	A	S	F	B	A	K	B
B	O	A	B	T	N	U	A	B	A	E
S	B	B	K	C	B	B	N	N	M	E
B	A	F	F	I	N	B	A	Y	D	T
I	N	O	N	D	N	H	N	R	E	N
G	D	A	P	E	I	G	A	R	B	O
B	A	Y	O	N	E	T	A	E	R	R
O	I	T	E	E	E	L	B	B	U	B
Y	D	B	E	B	A	Z	O	O	K	A

SCORING

Your answers (1 pt. each) _____

Matching answers
in the grid (1 pt. each) _____

Matching answers
in the hidden message
(2 pts. each) _____

GRAND TOTAL _____

SCATTERGORIES

Starting letter: I

1 Sports
_____
_____

2 Song Titles
_____
_____

3 Parts of the Body
_____
_____

4 Ethnic Foods
_____
_____

5 Things You Shout
_____
_____

6 Animals
_____
_____

7 U.S. States
_____
_____

8 Bands
_____
_____

9 Ways to Get From Here to There
_____
_____

10 Villains/Monsters
_____
_____

11 Media Technology
_____
_____

12 Found in a Hospital
_____
_____

Word List on page 155

Answer on page 138

```
R  E  G  N  I  F  X  E  D  N  I
A  G  E  I  N  S  T  E  P  I  V
C  A  N  R  E  T  N  I  I  N  A
A  S  O  T  N  O  S  N  E  T  N
N  U  H  N  G  I  U  L  T  H  T
I  A  P  A  W  B  L  I  A  E  H
N  S  I  F  E  E  N  N  T  N  E
S  N  I  N  T  X  I  E  S  A  T
U  A  N  I  S  I  N  S  R  V  E
L  I  C  E  H  O  C  K  E  Y  R
T  L  I  V  S  H  U  A  T  S  R
I  A  O  T  I  A  B  T  N  A  I
U  T  W  M  R  D  U  I  I  E  B
Q  I  A  U  I  I  S  N  B  M  L
I  X  E  A  N  A  U  G  I  I  E
```

SCATTERGORIES

Starting letter: O

1 Breakfast Foods

_____

_____

2 Famous Duos and Trios

_____

_____

3 Clothing Brands

_____

_____

4 Vacation Spots

_____

_____

5 Things in a Church

_____

_____

6 Words Associated
With Money

_____

_____

7 Items in a Vending
Machine

_____

_____

8 Movie Titles

_____

_____

9 Games

_____

_____

10 Things You Wear

_____

_____

11 Beers

_____

_____

12 Things at a Circus

_____

_____

Word List on page 156   Answer on page 138

```
O  X  F  O  R  D  S  Y  A  J  O
N  L  O  P  O  O  E  O  R  A  P
T  S  D  A  R  L  Y  R  H  T  E
H  L  H  M  L  D  V  A  A  A  R
E  U  T  O  A  M  A  N  B  O  A
W  O  P  E  N  I  N  G  A  C  T
A  D  W  I  D  L  D  E  L  R  I
T  O  H  E  O  W  L  P  A  E  O
E  R  O  S  D  A  O  O  E  V  N
R  E  V  E  O  U  R  P  M  O  O
F  O  O  U  T  K  A  S  T  R  I
R  S  S  H  N  E  H  O  A  G  T
O  O  M  E  L  E  T  S  O  A  A
N  E  M  N  O  I  T  P  O  N  V
T  O  S  G  N  I  R  E  F  F  O
```

SCATTERGORIES

Starting letter: D

1 Vegetables

7 Types of Drink

2 States

8 Musical Groups

3 Things You Throw Away

9 Store/Business Names

4 Occupations

10 Things at a Football Game

5 Appliances

11 Trees

6 Cartoon Characters

12 Personality Traits

Word List on page 157

Answer on page 139

D	E	C	I	D	U	O	U	S	D	E
A	P	S	D	I	L	L	A	R	D	S
N	A	I	R	A	D	R	Y	E	R	U
D	S	N	W	O	D	T	D	P	A	Y
E	D	A	I	K	O	N	E	A	W	G
L	R	O	T	C	O	D	C	I	P	N
I	I	R	I	U	Q	I	A	D	L	I
O	A	D	A	D	W	G	F	Y	A	R
N	P	D	E	D	K	N	Y	T	Y	E
G	S	D	E	L	A	W	A	R	E	E
R	E	H	S	A	W	H	S	I	D	N
E	D	X	G	N	I	R	A	D	T	I
E	E	R	D	O	G	W	O	O	D	M
N	O	V	E	D	A	N	C	E	R	O
S	E	L	B	A	S	O	P	S	I	D

SCATTERGORIES

Starting letter: C

1 Things at a Picnic

_____

_____

2 Things That Are Soft

_____

_____

3 Things in a Science
Fiction Movie

_____

_____

4 Things at the White
House

_____

_____

5 Things That Kids Play
With

_____

_____

6 Things at a Wedding

_____

_____

7 Hot Places

_____

_____

8 Things in Outer Space

_____

_____

9 Found in a Dorm

_____

_____

10 Found on a Ship

_____

_____

11 Famous Singers

_____

_____

12 Things at an
Amusement Park

_____

_____

Word List on page 158   Answer on page 139

C	T	E	S	S	S	E	H	C	O	W
F	N	R	E	T	U	P	M	O	C	E
F	C	O	N	T	R	O	L	L	E	R
A	S	H	O	R	I	A	C	L	R	C
T	E	N	I	B	A	C	A	E	E	A
S	C	T	H	P	A	L	P	G	M	K
F	H	A	S	R	S	E	T	E	O	E
O	E	E	U	E	L	S	A	S	N	L
F	R	S	C	L	A	U	I	T	Y	G
E	O	T	O	O	D	O	N	U	A	R
I	I	O	M	O	N	R	C	D	L	O
H	E	R	E	C	E	A	O	E	C	B
C	O	T	T	O	N	C	A	N	D	Y
E	H	P	O	R	T	S	A	T	A	C
S	S	Y	A	R	C	I	M	S	O	C

SCATTERGORIES

Starting letter: G

1 Worn Above the Waist
_____
_____

2 Things That Are Bright
_____
_____

3 Things That Have Numbers
_____
_____

4 Found in a Gym/Health Club
_____
_____

5 Things on a Safari
_____
_____

6 Ways to Say Hi and Bye
_____
_____

7 Things From the Sixties
_____
_____

8 Holiday Things
_____
_____

9 Items in an Office
_____
_____

10 Things in Pairs or Sets
_____
_____

11 Things on a Highway
_____
_____

12 Things in Las Vegas
_____
_____

Word List on page 159   Answer on page 139

```
G O L F C L U B S G S
Y D D U B D O O G U E
M G Y F S E V O L G M
N I L O G O O G A W A
A F G O H D N U O R G
S T O O B O G O K A
T S E Y X A L A G S S
S R E P A P H P A R G
D S I D E D I U G E U
N U A H Y G G R E U Z
A I G A S P U M P L Z
L N E E F F A R I G L
R E T A W D L O G T E
A G R I P S I O N G R
G G A M B L I N G S S
```

SCATTERGORIES

Starting letter: F

1 Pets
_____
_____

2 Things With Motors
_____
_____

3 Dances
_____
_____

4 Found at a Salad Bar
_____
_____

5 Football Terms
_____
_____

6 Found in the Woods
_____
_____

7 Things in a Hotel
_____
_____

8 Math Terms
_____
_____

9 Illumination Sources
_____
_____

10 Things in a Parade
_____
_____

11 Reasons to Skip School/Work
_____
_____

12 Titles People Have
_____
_____

Word List on page 150   Answer on page 140

```
F  O  R  R  R  E  H  S  I  F  M
G  A  N  E  L  B  M  U  F  I  F
A  F  V  P  T  T  A  G  F  R  L
L  E  T  A  T  E  U  N  A  S  A
F  H  O  P  E  R  R  U  C  T  S
F  L  R  S  F  R  L  F  T  L  H
F  F  T  W  I  E  E  L  O  I  L
D  O  X  E  I  F  L  A  R  E  I
F  R  O  N  T  D  E  S  K  U  G
M  K  F  E  R  R  A  R  I  T  H
F  I  R  E  E  N  G  I  N  E  T
A  F  I  R  S  T  D  O  W  N  R
D  O  O  F  E  U  G  I  T  A  F
S  H  F  R  A  C  T  I  O  N  A
L  F  O  O  T  P  R  I  N  T  S
```

SCATTERGORIES

Starting letter: K & V

1 Birds

_____

_____

2 Things in a Mystery
Novel

_____

_____

3 Computer Lingo

_____

_____

4 Loud Sounds

_____

_____

5 Articles of Clothing

_____

_____

6 Pro Sports Team
Names

_____

_____

7 Musical Instruments

_____

_____

8 Flavorings

_____

_____

9 Things in an Airport

_____

_____

10 Colleges/Universities

_____

_____

11 Things You Look
Through

_____

_____

12 Classic Rock Bands

_____

_____

Word List on page 151   Answer on page 140

```
N K K S O I K I A N G
E W F M I A S L H E R
L O Y O Z R O K K K A
A P R O K I L T O A S
H A O R V K I S S L S
N K M V E N E S H E A
A R E D N I F W E I V
V L M N T C I R R D U
I E L I T K N L S O L
K K A I T S K O A S T
I O U K N C T A L C U
N B T U I A I A T O R
G R R W R A V V T P E
S K I L O B Y T E E V
I K V A L I S E R E O
```

SCATTERGORIES

Starting letter: E

1 Boys' Names
_____
_____

2 U.S. Cities
_____
_____

3 Things That Are Cold
_____
_____

4 Art Class Supplies
_____
_____

5 Pro Sports Teams
_____
_____

6 Occupations
_____
_____

7 Breakfast Foods
_____
_____

8 Furniture
_____
_____

9 TV Shows
_____
_____

10 Things Found in the Ocean
_____
_____

11 Body Parts
_____
_____

12 Brand Names
_____
_____

Word List on page 152   Answer on page 140

```
E  L  E  C  T  R  I  C  E  E  L
S  W  O  B  L  E  E  R  N  I  E
R  E  T  H  A  S  E  E  G  D  N
E  A  S  T  L  A  N  S  I  N  G
L  T  N  E  G  R  D  K  N  A  L
I  E  A  L  L  E  T  I  E  L  I
O  P  E  G  G  V  A  M  E  S  S
N  S  A  G  E  E  B  O  R  I  H
O  O  S  I  O  R  L  P  E  R  M
T  N  E  T  E  E  I  L  E  U
N  E  L  P  A  S  O  E  L  T  F
O  D  D  R  O  T  I  D  E  S  F
M  C  I  R  E  X  X  O  N  A  I
D  S  U  G  A  H  P  O  S  E  N
E  N  T  O  U  R  A  G  E  I  E
```

SCATTERGORIES

Starting letter: A

1 Famous Females

_____

_____

2 Medicine/Drugs

_____

_____

3 Things Made of Metal

_____

_____

4 Hobbies

_____

_____

5 Bands

_____

_____

6 Things You Plug In

_____

_____

7 Animals

_____

_____

8 Languages

_____

_____

9 Names of People in the Bible

_____

_____

10 Healthy Foods

_____

_____

11 Things That Grow

_____

_____

12 Companies

_____

_____

Word List on page 153

Answer on page 141

```
S  C  I  T  S  O  R  C  A  A  S
Y  P  A  K  R  A  V  D  R  A  A
L  A  N  L  I  A  L  E  R  R  M
P  D  N  R  F  N  N  P  M  I  E
P  I  N  G  O  A  A  E  A  D  L
U  D  V  I  L  C  N  L  A  C  I
S  A  P  P  L  I  A  N  C  E  A
R  S  R  N  A  N  N  I  T  I  E
I  I  H  N  I  S  B  G  S  T  A
A  I  D  A  T  A  P  P  L  E  R
D  A  A  E  R  O  S  M  I  T  H
A  M  S  A  I  N  E  V  E  L  A
M  S  A  M  P  L  I  F  I  E  R
A  S  P  A  R  A  G  U  S  B  T
E  L  I  B  O  M  O  T  U  A  E
```

SCATTERGORIES

Starting letter: B

1 Articles of Clothing
_____
_____

2 Desserts
_____
_____

3 Car Parts
_____
_____

4 Nations of the New World
_____
_____

5 Athletes
_____
_____

6 Things at a Circus
_____
_____

7 Items in a Refrigerator
_____
_____

8 Farm Animals
_____
_____

9 Street Names
_____
_____

10 Things at the Beach
_____
_____

11 Colors
_____
_____

12 Tools
_____
_____

Word List on page 154   Answer on page 141

```
B  L  I  N  K  E  R  B  L  A  K
A  R  E  T  T  U  C  T  L  O  B
S  B  O  U  R  B  O  N  U  B  R
E  B  R  A  Z  I  L  T  B  I  E
B  A  K  E  D  A  L  A  S  K  A
A  O  B  L  P  W  B  O  N  I  D
L  A  L  A  O  A  A  G  O  N  P
L  D  U  O  T  S  V  Y  O  I  U
P  U  E  T  G  D  A  L  L  B  D
L  M  E  B  I  N  I  L  L  U  D
A  R  B  S  B  A  A  I  A  T  I
Y  E  O  S  U  B  C  B  B  T  N
E  B  X  O  B  O  W  T  I  E  G
R  T  E  K  N  A  L  B  T  R  T
B  U  R  N  T  U  M  B  E  R  I
```

SCATTERGORIES

Starting letter: W

1 Superheroes
_____
_____

2 Presents
_____
_____

3 Birds
_____
_____

4 Kinds of Dances
_____
_____

5 Things That Are Black
_____
_____

6 Vehicles
_____
_____

7 Tropical Locations
_____
_____

8 College Majors
_____
_____

9 Dairy Products
_____
_____

10 Things in a Church
_____
_____

11 Best Actor/Actress
Oscar Winners
_____
_____

12 Sports
_____
_____

Word List on page 155

Answer on page 141

W	E	D	D	I	N	G	G	I	F	T
W	E	N	I	R	E	V	L	O	W	I
N	E	B	D	J	W	W	A	M	M	M
W	O	N	D	E	R	W	O	M	A	N
H	E	O	I	E	E	S	A	R	E	W
I	T	L	N	W	S	E	N	T	R	T
P	I	O	R	A	T	I	O	E	C	A
P	U	P	Z	T	L	D	G	G	G	H
O	S	R	T	U	I	N	A	N	N	S
O	T	E	L	S	N	I	W	I	I	H
R	E	T	A	I	G	T	C	T	P	C
W	W	A	W	A	R	S	H	I	P	T
I	H	W	W	A	F	E	R	R	I	I
L	E	E	N	Y	A	W	K	W	H	W
L	Y	E	I	K	I	K	I	A	W	R

SCATTERGORIES

Starting letter: T

1 Sandwiches

_____

_____

2 Items in a Catalog

_____

_____

3 World Leaders/
Politicians

_____

_____

4 School Subjects

_____

_____

5 Excuses for Being Late

_____

_____

6 Ice Cream Flavors

_____

_____

7 Animated Disney
Movie Characters

_____

_____

8 Television Stars

_____

_____

9 Things in a Park

_____

_____

10 Foreign Cities

_____

_____

11 Stones/Gems

_____

_____

12 Musical Instruments

_____

_____

Word List on page 156   Answer on page 142

```
K  T  E  D  K  E  N  N  E  D  Y
E  O  T  G  N  I  P  Y  T  E  L
B  O  A  I  T  L  V  E  A  I  T
E  K  T  R  U  L  V  K  L  R  R
R  A  I  T  T  E  T  R  O  E  U
T  W  G  U  T  B  E  U  C  T  M
E  R  G  B  I  R  S  T  O  T  P
D  O  E  A  F  E  I  R  H  O  E
D  N  R  E  R  K  O  E  C  T  T
A  G  A  S  U  N  U  H  E  R  R
N  T  Z  Y  T  I  Q  C  L  E  A
S  U  A  O  T  T  R  T  P  T  F
O  R  P  T  I  I  U  A  I  E  F
N  N  O  Y  K  O  T  H  R  E  I
P  E  T  U  N  A  I  T  T  T  C
```

SCATTERGORIES

Starting letter: M

1 Nicknames

_____

_____

2 Things in the Sky

_____

_____

3 Pizza Toppings

_____

_____

4 Colleges/Universities

_____

_____

5 Fish

_____

_____

6 Countries

_____

_____

7 Things That Have Spots

_____

_____

8 Historical Figures

_____

_____

9 Things You Might Be Afraid Of

_____

_____

10 Terms of Measurement

_____

_____

11 Brand Names

_____

_____

12 Book Titles

_____

_____

Word List on page 157   Answer on page 142

```
A  L  L  E  R  A  Z  Z  O  M  E
M  A  C  I  N  T  O  S  H  E  K
A  M  A  M  H  M  I  E  T  A  O
D  M  A  A  H  C  K  K  O  S  Y
A  L  E  R  E  K  C  A  M  L  L
M  M  I  C  M  I  I  T  E  E  O
E  I  M  O  E  N  D  S  T  S  H
B  L  A  N  R  L  Y  I  E  S  T
O  E  C  I  M  E  B  M  R  U  N
V  L  R  A  I  Y  O  G  N  F  U
A  M  N  O  I  O  M  N  N  F  O
R  N  K  M  E  O  C  I  X  E  M
Y  F  A  I  O  T  S  K  K  R  A
M  I  N  N  O  W  E  A  H  E  L
M  U  S  H  R  O  O  M  S  R  I
```

SCATTERGORIES

Starting letter: H

1 Fictional Characters

_____

_____

2 Cookout Foods

_____

_____

3 Things You Shout

_____

_____

4 Capitals

_____

_____

5 Sweets

_____

_____

6 Items You Save Up to Buy

_____

_____

7 Footwear

_____

_____

8 Things You Keep Hidden

_____

_____

9 Authors

_____

_____

10 Things With Tails

_____

_____

11 Sports Equipment

_____

_____

12 Crimes

_____

_____

Word List on page 158

Answer on page 142

```
H  H  U  C  H  E  L  M  E  T  K
H  O  C  K  E  Y  S  T  I  C  K
E  Y  H  O  U  S  E  A  F  E  I
A  E  A  A  O  N  N  N  R  N  H
L  H  M  W  R  H  O  A  A  R  S
T  O  B  P  G  E  T  T  B  O  E
H  M  U  H  L  N  L  N  H  H  L
P  I  R  O  O  E  I  O  T  T  U
R  C  G  T  I  O  H  M  A  W  C
O  I  E  D  P  V  R  H  E  A  R
B  D  R  O  F  T  R  A  H  H  E
L  E  S  G  H  D  O  N  Y  U  H
E  S  L  E  E  H  A  N  O  I  L
M  I  N  U  R  D  N  A  T  I  H
S  P  O  T  H  G  I  H  H  A  N
```

SCATTERGORIES

Starting letter: N

1 Things That Are Sticky

_____

_____

2 Awards/Ceremonies

_____

_____

3 Cars

_____

_____

4 Seen in the Night Sky

_____

_____

5 Personality Traits

_____

_____

6 Cosmetics/Toiletries

_____

_____

7 Celebrities

_____

_____

8 Synonyms for "Zero"

_____

_____

9 Infamous Leaders

_____

_____

10 Fictional Places

_____

_____

11 Leisure Activities

_____

_____

12 Things People Write

_____

_____

Word List on page 159   Answer on page 143

```
N  N  N  I  N  I  S  S  A  N  C
E  E  I  A  E  N  U  T  P  E  N
S  N  N  O  S  L  O  H  C  I  N
T  A  T  Y  N  H  S  G  T  A  R
L  Y  E  D  N  A  A  I  I  I  I
E  V  N  E  V  E  R  L  A  N  D
C  E  D  E  N  N  P  N  O  A  N
A  N  O  N  U  O  L  R  I  D  A
N  O  B  E  L  R  T  E  C  A  P
D  O  M  I  N  N  O  H  V  M  P
Y  I  S  T  O  I  T  T  I  O  I
B  H  N  T  A  L  M  R  I  N  N
A  N  E  T  A  G  U  O  N  C  G
R  Y  R  E  B  W  E  N  Y  O  R
M  N  O  E  L  O  P  A  N  A  L
```

SCATTERGORIES

Starting letter: C

1 Restaurants
_____
_____

2 Notorious People
_____
_____

3 Fruits
_____
_____

4 Things in a Medicine Cabinet
_____
_____

5 Games/Playthings
_____
_____

6 Household Chores
_____
_____

7 Bodies of Water
_____
_____

8 Authors
_____
_____

9 Halloween Costumes
_____
_____

10 Weapons
_____

11 Things That Are Round
_____
_____

12 Words Associated With Exercise
_____
_____

Word List on page 150   Answer on page 143

A	L	A	N	A	C	O	N	R	A	D
E	G	N	I	K	O	O	C	I	C	A
S	C	A	P	O	N	E	H	P	O	O
N	T	R	G	N	I	N	A	E	L	C
A	V	C	A	C	H	E	R	R	Y	O
I	O	A	T	N	W	O	L	C	E	U
P	H	S	E	E	I	C	E	H	S	G
S	K	A	A	D	L	U	S	U	U	H
A	E	B	R	C	E	P	M	R	O	S
C	H	A	T	T	Y	C	A	T	H	Y
C	C	H	I	L	I	S	N	C	B	R
B	P	M	A	R	C	A	S	M	A	U
U	U	S	C	C	O	L	O	L	R	P
A	L	L	E	R	E	D	N	I	C	I
N	E	S	C	R	O	S	S	B	O	W

SCORING

Your answers (1 pt. each) _____

Matching answers
in the grid (1 pt. each) _____

Matching answers
in the hidden message
(2 pts. each) _____

GRAND TOTAL _____

SCATTERGORIES

Starting letter: F

1 Sports

_____

_____

2 Song Titles

_____

_____

3 Parts of the Body

_____

_____

4 Ethnic Foods

_____

_____

5 Things You Shout

_____

_____

6 Birds

_____

_____

7 Girls' Names

_____

_____

8 Ways to Get From Here to There

_____

_____

9 Items in the Kitchen

_____

_____

10 Villains/Monsters

_____

_____

11 Flowers

_____

_____

12 Things You Replace

_____

_____

Word List on page 151   Answer on page 143

```
F  O  O  T  L  O  O  S  E  Y  F
F  I  R  E  U  N  G  F  F  E  U
H  C  N  I  F  N  N  F  R  K  U
F  N  F  G  R  L  I  L  A  C  A
F  O  R  G  E  T  M  E  N  O  T
L  U  R  S  E  R  A  N  K  H  A
E  E  N  K  W  F  L  N  E  D  T
U  C  E  K  A  O  F  U  N  L  A
R  A  C  H  Y  O  D  F  S  E  T
D  F  A  J  I  T  A  N  T  I  T
E  D  N  A  N  B  O  C  E  F  I
L  F  R  I  D  A  E  W  I  I  R
I  A  U  F  T  L  E  B  N  A  F
S  S  F  F  E  L  I  C  I  A  A
M  T  H  G  I  F  D  O  O  F  E
```

SCATTERGORIES

Starting letter: J

1 Months
_____
_____

2 Musical Groups
_____
_____

3 Things You Throw
_____
_____

4 Vacation Spots
_____
_____

5 Comedians
_____
_____

6 Dances*
_____
_____

7 Items in a Vending
Machine
_____
_____

8 Movie Titles
_____
_____

9 Flowers
_____
_____

10 Body Parts
_____
_____

11 TV Families
_____
_____

12 Occupations
_____
_____

Word List on page 152   Answer on page 144

```
J U J U N K F O O D R
A O E R A L U G U J S
S N R I A C I A M A J
J E R S E Y S H O R E
I L Y L U J U N E T T
G Y S D D U J C L S H
P A E A J G S R I K R
J J I A A U N Z U J O
I J N Z V B O J Q A T
J E F F E R S O N S U
N W E S L E T I O M L
A E L S I T E N J I L
M L D W N T J T I N N
U E J A N I T O R E G
J R E J U J U B E S R
```

SCATTERGORIES

Starting letter: O

1 Vegetables

_____

_____

2 U.S. States

_____

_____

3 Found in the Ocean

_____

_____

4 Occupations

_____

_____

5 Appliances

_____

_____

6 Cartoon Characters

_____

_____

7 Types of Drink

_____

_____

8 Male Singers

_____

_____

9 Awards/Ceremonies

_____

_____

10 Football Terms

_____

_____

11 Trees*

_____

_____

12 Personality Traits

_____

_____

Word List on page 153   Answer on page 144

```
O O R E G O N F F O S
I V O E N D O S C A R
E E S D I O O T T O E
F R T N T V O F K E Z
N T E O T P I R K Y I
S I N M U N A L A L R
A M T S P Y E O O R E
M E A O F G P E A E T
O U T O F B O U N D S
H N I G O O R R I R O
A N O I N O U E G O C
L E U I V O R A N G E
K V S E B E L R A O F
O F N S I C I O R C A
A L O O L I V E O Y L
```

SCORING

Your answers (1 pt. each) _____

Matching answers
in the grid (1 pt. each) _____

Matching answers
in the hidden message
(2 pts. each) _____

GRAND TOTAL _____

SCATTERGORIES

Starting letter: R

1 Things You Listen to

_____

_____

2 Things That Are Soft

_____

_____

3 Things in a Science
Fiction Movie

_____

_____

4 Things at the White
House

_____

_____

5 Things That Kids Play
With

_____

_____

6 Things at a Wedding

_____

_____

7 Hot Places

_____

_____

8 Fictional Characters

_____

_____

9 Found in a Dorm

_____

10 Sandwiches

_____

_____

11 Famous Singers

_____

_____

12 Things at an
Amusement Park

_____

_____

Word List on page 154

Answer on page 144

```
R  U  B  B  E  R  B  A  L  L  R
P  I  H  S  T  E  K  C  O  R  R
M  E  Y  A  R  O  M  E  O  I  O
A  D  N  A  W  R  R  T  N  D  L
L  I  R  E  D  Y  O  A  E  D  L
G  R  O  B  S  H  N  M  D  L  E
N  E  B  U  E  R  S  M  R  E  R
I  C  O  C  M  D  T  O  A  R  C
D  O  T  S  I  A  A  O  G  A  O
A  R  V  K  R  S  D  R  E  D  A
E  D  I  I  T  E  T  S  S  I  S
R  A  B  B  I  T  S  F  O  O  T
R  I  E  U  A  G  N  I  R  I  E
T  E  C  R  E  C  L  I  N  E  R
F  S  R  E  T  R  O  P  E  R  T
```

SCATTERGORIES

Starting letter: L

1 Worn Above the Waist
_____
_____

2 Things That Are Bright
_____
_____

3 Things That Have Numbers
_____
_____

4 Found in a Gym/Health Club
_____
_____

5 Things on a Safari
_____
_____

6 Ways to Say Hi and Bye
_____
_____

7 Things From the Sixties
_____
_____

8 Holiday Things
_____
_____

9 Items in an Office
_____
_____

10 Things in Pairs or Sets
_____
_____

11 Things on a Highway
_____
_____

12 Things in Las Vegas
_____

Word List on page 155   Answer on page 145

```
L L O N G H A I R E A
V N E L E X U S A N A
S O L N E G D O L A T
G S A E S N E C I L N
N N S M O E P L I A A
U H U R N G S P S H S
L O C K E R S I R L O
N J L S M T D L E E T
N B L E I S F B S P S
R N N C T O A I O M R
E O K N G L N T L A E
T D X L N I P O B L T
A N E U O A T R I A T
L Y T I L T H G I L E
O L A B O R D A Y N L
```

SCATTERGORIES

Starting letter: T

1 Things at a Zoo

_____

_____

2 Things With Motors

_____

_____

3 Native American Things

_____

_____

4 Chemical Elements

_____

_____

5 Words Ending in "LY"

_____

_____

6 Things on a Hiking Trip

_____

_____

7 Things in a Hotel

_____

_____

8 Healthy Foods

_____

_____

9 Found in a Classroom

_____

_____

10 Party Things

_____

11 Reasons to Skip School/Work

_____

_____

12 Things on Kids' Bikes

_____

_____

Word List on page 156   Answer on page 145

```
T  I  T  A  N  I  U  M  T  E  T
R  R  E  C  T  R  A  C  T  O  R
A  H  A  T  U  N  G  S  T  E  N
I  N  C  V  I  C  A  A  O  T  E
N  L  H  U  E  E  L  S  R  A  M
I  L  E  T  F  L  Y  E  T  S  E
N  K  R  O  Y  O  E  E  O  S  H
G  T  O  Y  R  P  T  R  I  E  T
W  L  U  O  E  M  L  T  S  L  E
H  Y  I  T  B  E  T  R  E  S  R
E  H  C  A  H  T  O  O  T  L  R
E  U  S  T  R  O  X  I  N  E  I
L  T  O  M  A  T  O  E  G  W  B
S  S  E  N  D  E  R  I  T  O  L
G  L  T  R  E  A  T  S  Y  T  Y
```

SCATTERGORIES

Starting letter: G

1 Desert Areas
_____
_____

2 Things in a Mystery Novel
_____
_____

3 Things on the Internet
_____
_____

4 Loud Things
_____
_____

5 Kinds of Soups/Stews
_____
_____

6 Math Terms
_____
_____

7 Underground Things
_____
_____

8 Things in the Wild West
_____

9 Things in an Airport
_____

10 Flowers/Plants
_____

11 Found in New York City
_____

12 Things in Fairy Tales
_____

Word List on page 157   Answer on page 145

```
G  A  N  N  I  L  B  O  G  A  G
G  G  U  G  G  E  N  H  E  I  M
G  I  Z  A  U  H  O  S  R  N  G
G  O  D  Z  I  L  L  A  A  E  R
U  T  T  P  L  O  C  E  N  D  O
N  W  N  A  T  R  L  H  I  R  U
S  O  G  C  E  G  O  L  U  A  N
L  T  D  H  O  O  M  G  M  G  D
I  T  P  O  K  B  I  R  N  E  C
N  O  G  E  E  I  G  E  E  D  O
G  R  E  A  T  E  R  T  H  A  N
E  G  U  M  B  O  A  E  G  N  T
R  E  R  O  N  G  P  L  I  E  R
M  O  G  U  M  S  H  O  E  R  O
B  M  O  T  S  T  N  A  R  G  L
```

SCATTERGORIES

Starting letter: H

1 Boys' Names

2 U.S. Cities

3 Things That Are Cold

4 School Supplies

5 Pro Sports Teams

6 Insects

7 Breakfast Foods

8 Furniture

9 TV Shows

10 Fish

11 Presidents

12 Parts of a Ship

Word List on page 158   Answer on page 146

```
S  H  A  P  P  Y  D  A  Y  S  H
N  H  O  O  T  U  B  I  L  A  H
W  H  O  U  S  T  O  N  R  N  A
O  E  Y  M  S  E  O  R  E  H  W
R  H  O  C  K  E  Y  R  I  N  K
B  O  H  A  R  D  F  A  C  T  S
H  H  C  N  U  P  E  L  O  H  O
S  G  N  E  L  R  S  H  Y  O  H
A  N  A  H  U  T  C  H  R  N  A
H  I  G  H  L  I  G  H  T  E  R
E  R  H  O  O  V  E  R  T  Y  R
N  R  U  T  N  O  T  H  A  B  I
R  E  L  H  O  T  C  A  K  E  S
Y  H  L  R  H  E  L  M  E  E  O
T  D  R  A  O  B  D  A  E  H  N
```

SCORING

Your answers (1 pt. each)	_____
Matching answers in the grid (1 pt. each)	_____
Matching answers in the hidden message (2 pts. each)	_____
GRAND TOTAL	_____

SCATTERGORIES

Starting letter: P

1 Famous Females

_____

_____

2 Medicine/Drugs

_____

_____

3 Things Made of Metal

_____

_____

4 Hobbies

_____

_____

5 People in Uniform

_____

_____

6 Things You Plug In

_____

_____

7 Animals

_____

_____

8 Languages

_____

_____

9 Names of People in the Bible

_____

_____

10 Junk Food

_____

_____

11 Things That Grow

_____

_____

12 Companies

_____

_____

Word List on page 159   Answer on page 146

```
P  P  I  L  C  R  E  P  A  P  H
P  O  P  T  A  R  T  O  O  L  P
R  R  I  X  I  V  A  L  P  E  A
U  T  N  P  R  A  I  I  R  Z  O
D  U  O  A  R  S  L  C  R  T  Y
E  G  C  R  H  O  O  E  H  E  H
N  U  C  R  T  L  Z  M  P  R  P
T  E  H  O  A  I  P  A  O  P  A
I  S  I  T  F  P  A  N  C  E  R
A  E  O  P  A  I  N  T  I  N  G
L  R  S  N  D  C  D  T  S  O  O
U  E  N  I  N  K  O  U  O  H  T
A  T  O  S  A  A  R  P  L  P  O
P  E  S  I  P  X  A  L  E  A  H
T  P  E  E  S  E  I  P  P  O  P
```

SCATTERGORIES

Starting letter: I

1 Money Lingo

_____

_____

2 Desserts

_____

_____

3 Car Parts

_____

_____

4 Countries

_____

_____

5 Athletes

_____

_____

6 Things in a Medicine Cabinet

_____

_____

7 Seen in the Arctic

_____

_____

8 MP3 Player Lingo

_____

_____

9 Girls' Names

_____

_____

10 Baseball Terms

_____

_____

11 Colors

_____

_____

12 Classic TV Shows

_____

_____

Word List on page 150   Answer on page 146

```
D  I  N  I  S  L  A  N  D  E  R
L  T  L  D  N  E  L  N  A  V  I
E  E  R  E  E  N  I  D  O  I  S
I  T  A  L  I  A  N  I  C  E  I
F  R  I  B  U  P  R  O  F  E  N
N  T  E  I  I  T  U  N  E  S  V
I  I  N  N  I  N  G  R  I  D  E
L  M  C  N  E  E  D  F  L  I  S
O  A  P  E  T  M  I  I  N  Y  T
V  O  O  O  C  U  O  U  G  R  M
E  N  L  I  R  R  I  C  N  O  E
L  S  Y  G  I  T  E  R  N  V  N
U  D  P  E  I  S  R  A  A  I  T
C  T  S  R  A  N  R  D  M  Q  I
Y  N  I  G  N  I  T  I  O  N  G
```

SCATTERGORIES

Starting letter: L

1 Heroes

_____

_____

2 Gifts/Presents

_____

_____

3 Terms of Endearment

_____

_____

4 Kinds of Dances

_____

_____

5 Things That Are Black

_____

_____

6 Vehicles

_____

_____

7 Tropical Locations

_____

_____

8 College Majors

_____

_____

9 Dairy Products

_____

_____

10 Living Spaces

_____

_____

11 Items in Your Purse/Wallet

_____

_____

12 Sports

_____

_____

Word List on page 151   Answer on page 147

```
L  L  L  A  S  P  A  L  M  A  S
I  O  E  S  N  E  C  I  L  T  S
T  R  E  I  R  E  G  N  I  L  O
E  D  N  I  B  A  C  G  O  L  L
J  N  L  O  N  G  J  U  M  P  G
R  E  G  R  U  B  M  I  L  E  P
A  L  A  C  R  O  S  S  E  N  I
E  S  R  P  L  O  F  T  A  I  L
L  O  W  F  A  T  M  I  L  K  I
E  N  L  T  T  C  U  C  O  B  M
A  R  O  A  I  E  S  S  C  M  O
T  L  V  I  N  B  E  N  K  A  B
H  R  E  A  L  A  A  R  E  L  M
E  T  Y  Y  D  N  I  L  T  L  I
R  S  D  R  A  U  G  E  F  I  L
```

SCATTERGORIES

Starting letter: J

1 Foods
_____
_____

2 Items in a Catalog
_____
_____

3 World Leaders/
Politicians
_____
_____

4 School Subjects
_____
_____

5 Excuses for Being Late
_____
_____

6 Christmas Carols
_____
_____

7 Things That
Jump/Bounce
_____
_____

8 Television Stars
_____
_____

9 Adverbs
_____
_____

10 Festive Occasions
_____
_____

11 Stones/Gems
_____
_____

12 Musicians
_____
_____

Word List on page 152   Answer on page 147

```
J  M  S  I  L  A  N  R  U  O  J
J  O  G  G  E  R  J  E  N  G  O
J  O  E  B  I  D  E  N  O  A  Y
R  K  Y  L  T  S  U  J  S  L  T
J  O  N  S  T  E  W  A  R  T  O
J  O  L  L  E  J  E  G  E  E  T
A  Y  E  L  K  E  E  G  F  J  H
C  T  W  E  C  E  R  E  F  E  E
K  U  E  B  A  L  O  R  E  R  W
R  D  J  E  J  I  B  Y  J  S  O
A  Y  A  L  A  B  M  A  J  E  R
B  R  D  G  J  U  A  A  R  Y  L
B  U  E  N  L  J  J  U  D  O  D
I  J  O  I  N  T  L  Y  S  B  E
T  R  G  J  O  Y  B  E  H  A  R
```

SCORING

Your answers (1 pt. each) _____

Matching answers
in the grid (1 pt. each) _____

Matching answers
in the hidden message
(2 pts. each) _____

GRAND TOTAL _____

115

SCATTERGORIES

Starting letter: A

1 Nicknames

_____

_____

2 Things in the Sky

_____

_____

3 Vegetables

_____

_____

4 Colleges/Universities

_____

_____

5 Fish

_____

_____

6 Countries

_____

_____

7 Things That Have Spots

_____

_____

8 Historical Figures

_____

_____

9 Things You Might Be
Afraid Of

_____

_____

10 Terms of Measurement

_____

_____

11 Items in a Living Room

_____

_____

12 Book Titles

_____

_____

Word List on page 153

Answer on page 147

```
A P P A L O O S A A L
C M R A F L A M I N A
N A R T I C H O K E N
E V Y A E E I N N A N
S A B V R A A M A R A
U L S S O A R A R C K
F A T P C H M A I H A
F N N R A T C G E I R
E C E A B R H N S M E
R H I U L O A I A E N
E E C B A L I G H D I
R A D U P E R A U E N
E L P R Y A R T H S A
H A I N A B L A L E X
I A N G O L A D A M S
```

SCATTERGORIES

Starting letter: K & U

1 Fictional Characters

_____

_____

2 Menu Items

_____

_____

3 Worn Around the Waist

_____

_____

4 World Capitals

_____

_____

5 Kinds of Candy

_____

_____

6 Companies

_____

_____

7 Footwear

_____

_____

8 Actresses

_____

_____

9 U.S. States

_____

_____

10 Things With Tails

_____

_____

11 Sports Equipment

_____

_____

12 Crimes

_____

_____

Word List on page 154   Answer on page 148

```
K  O  K  E  N  T  U  C  K  Y  M
L  U  K  O  A  R  K  S  D  R  O
U  P  A  K  L  A  I  E  U  U  N
B  S  T  D  A  M  L  S  H  S  A
A  I  E  R  O  K  L  S  A  U  M
K  D  W  A  K  I  I  Y  U  G  R
A  E  I  O  N  N  N  L  L  O  U
Y  D  N  K  K  G  G  U  T  A  H
A  O  S  A  N  K  G  A  A  R  T
K  W  L  O  O  O  B  K  I  T  A
U  N  E  V  E  N  B  A  R  S  M
G  C  T  E  A  G  U  N  D  D  U
G  A  E  L  R  U  N  D  I  E  S
S  K  U  N  I  C  O  R  N  K  D
D  E  P  P  A  R  W  N  U  O  G
```

SCATTERGORIES

Starting letter: S

1 Things That Are Sticky

_____

_____

2 Awards/Ceremonies

_____

_____

3 Cars

_____

_____

4 Spices/Herbs

_____

_____

5 Bad Habits

_____

_____

6 Cosmetics/Toiletries

_____

_____

7 Celebrities

_____

_____

8 Kitchen Utensils

_____

_____

9 Reptiles/Amphibians

_____

_____

10 Cable TV Channels

_____

_____

11 Leisure Activities

_____

_____

12 Things That You're Allergic To

_____

_____

Word List on page 155   Answer on page 148

S	I	L	V	E	R	M	E	D	A	L
S	P	S	W	I	M	M	I	N	G	R
S	K	O	I	S	P	O	O	N	E	E
L	A	L	R	P	N	I	E	N	C	G
P	T	F	U	E	T	A	A	S	N	G
A	I	R	F	A	S	D	K	I	A	E
O	Y	H	U	R	E	A	K	E	D	N
S	S	T	S	S	O	O	S	M	N	E
L	I	A	A	R	M	N	A	I	U	Z
S	D	T	A	S	A	O	G	T	S	R
S	C	R	A	B	B	L	E	W	N	A
I	G	S	H	A	M	P	O	O	S	W
E	H	S	I	F	L	L	E	H	S	H
V	G	N	I	R	A	E	W	S	C	C
E	R	E	D	N	A	M	A	L	A	S

SCATTERGORIES

Starting letter: N

1 Brand Names

_____

_____

2 Notorious People

_____

_____

3 Fruits

_____

_____

4 Things in a Medicine
Cabinet

_____

_____

5 Toys

_____

_____

6 Home Activities

_____

_____

7 Bodies of Water

_____

_____

8 Authors

_____

_____

9 Halloween Costumes

_____

_____

10 Weapons

_____

_____

11 Things That Are Round

_____

_____

12 Words Associated
With Exercise

_____

_____

Word List on page 156   Answer on page 148

N	E	E	D	L	E	W	O	R	K	N
I	T	N	N	A	P	N	I	K	E	O
N	S	I	N	A	B	O	K	O	V	S
T	I	H	O	O	N	P	L	E	O	E
E	L	C	R	N	U	A	N	N	N	S
N	E	A	T	E	N	I	N	G	U	P
D	V	M	H	O	C	N	N	R	C	R
O	O	S	S	K	H	N	E	M	L	A
A	N	U	E	N	A	O	C	E	E	Y
N	O	L	A	I	K	G	T	S	A	S
E	D	I	N	L	U	A	A	R	R	I
S	O	T	S	E	N	I	R	U	B	Z
T	Z	U	A	T	E	N	I	N	J	A
L	L	A	B	F	R	E	N	E	S	N
E	G	N	A	R	O	L	E	V	A	N

SCATTERGORIES

Starting letter: E

1 Sports

_____

_____

2 Song Titles

_____

_____

3 Parts of the Body

_____

_____

4 Ethnic Foods

_____

_____

5 Things You Shout

_____

_____

6 Birds

_____

_____

7 Girls' Names

_____

_____

8 Ways to Get From Here
to There

_____

_____

9 Items in the Kitchen

_____

_____

10 Things You Give

_____

_____

11 Flowers

_____

_____

12 Things You Fix

_____

_____

Word List on page 157　　　　　　Answer on page 149

E	D	I	L	E	Y	E	L	I	V	E
Y	A	W	S	S	E	R	P	X	E	L
R	E	E	I	E	N	I	Z	E	A	E
O	M	Q	G	A	D	C	E	A	E	S
T	P	U	B	R	L	A	N	S	L	P
A	A	E	E	L	E	A	I	T	P	R
V	N	S	T	O	S	T	G	E	M	E
E	A	T	H	B	S	A	N	R	A	S
L	D	R	O	E	L	R	E	L	X	S
E	A	I	S	E	O	R	A	I	E	O
U	G	A	E	M	V	E	G	L	I	M
R	E	N	B	L	E	Y	L	Y	E	A
E	L	L	O	R	G	G	E	L	A	K
K	I	S	S	I	E	W	L	E	D	E
A	N	E	E	G	G	T	I	M	E	R

SCATTERGORIES

Starting letter: R

1 Things in a Child's Nursery

_____

_____

2 Famous Women

_____

_____

3 Things That Have Numbers

_____

_____

4 Things in a Gym

_____

_____

5 Things on a Safari

_____

_____

6 Vegetables

_____

_____

7 Things from the Sixties

_____

_____

8 Christmas Things

_____

_____

9 Presidents

_____

_____

10 Things at a County Fair

_____

_____

11 Things on a Highway

_____

_____

12 Music Genres

_____

_____

Word List on page 158

Answer on page 149

```
R  N  R  E  G  G  A  E  E  R  B
H  A  U  L  O  N  I  H  R  O  A
S  G  N  F  R  O  U  T  E  S  T
I  A  N  I  O  X  M  C  E  I  L
D  E  I  R  S  I  N  X  R  E  E
A  R  N  U  S  N  E  R  U  T  V
R  E  G  D  T  D  O  U  T  H  E
E  S  S  O  O  R  I  B  A  E  S
I  T  H  L  R  A  S  D  B  R  O
N  A  O  P  A  H  E  O  A  I  O
D  R  E  H  T  C  D  W  G  V  R
E  E  S  R  T  I  I  N  A  E  A
E  A  E  R  L  R  R  D  I  T  M
R  O  C  K  E  R  V  E  A  E  P
R  L  L  O  R  N  K  C  O  R  S
```

SCATTERGORIES

Starting letter: D

1 Things in a Desert

_____

_____

2 Things in a Mystery
Novel

_____

_____

3 Computer Lingo

_____

_____

4 Loud Things*

_____

_____

5 Things You Open

_____

_____

6 Math Terms

_____

_____

7 Underground Things

_____

_____

8 Things in the Wild West

_____

9 Airport Lingo

_____

10 Flowers

_____

11 Found in New York City

_____

12 Things in Fairy Tales

_____

Word List on page 159   Answer on page 149

```
D  D  D  R  O  M  E  D  A  R  Y
E  D  I  V  I  S  O  R  E  T  R
L  O  A  D  A  T  A  B  A  S  E
A  O  M  S  K  T  O  P  D  A  G
Y  R  E  W  A  R  D  I  S  L  N
D  E  T  E  C  T  I  V  E  B  I
O  D  E  P  A  R  T  U  R  E  R
B  P  R  L  A  N  Y  D  N  T  R
D  E  L  I  S  W  O  U  C  I  E
A  D  A  F  F  O  D  I  L  M  D
E  D  E  P  U  T  Y  S  I  A  D
D  I  A  M  O  N  D  M  I  N  E
D  A  O  L  N  W  O  D  U  Y  M
D  U  N  G  E  O  N  E  N  D  T
N  O  G  A  R  D  A  M  S  E  L
```

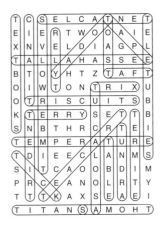

10-11

T
TV Shows

(THE) TWILIGHT ZONE
THREE'S COMPANY
TAXI

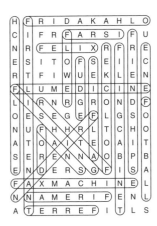

12-13

F
Things That Grow

FRUIT
FINGERNAILS

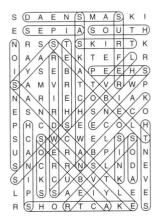

14-15

S
Athletes

SKIER
SKATER
(PETE) SAMPRAS
SOCCER PLAYER

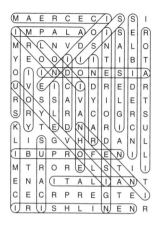

16-17

I
Occupations

INVESTIGATOR
INTERPRETER

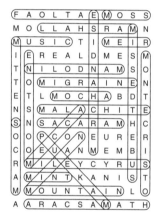

18-19

M
Foreign Cities

MONTREAL
MELBOURNE
MANILA

20-21

O
Book Titles

ORLANDO
OUR MUTUAL FRIEND

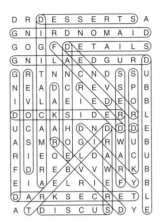

22-23

D
Things With Tails

DRAGON
DINGO
DEVIL RAY

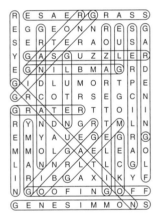

24-25

G
Cars

GENERAL MOTORS
GTO
GALAXY

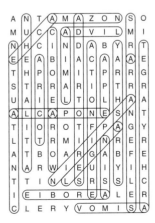

26-27

A
Weapons

ATOMIC BOMB
ARTILLERY

28-29

N
Girls' Names

NATALIE
NATASHA
NORA

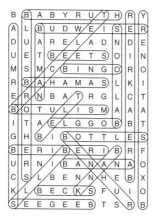

30-31

B
Words Associated With Money

BREAD
BARGAIN
BENEFITS

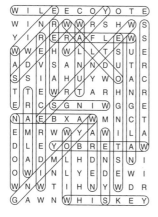

32-33

W
Personality Traits

WISHY-WASHY
WARM
WHINY
WITHDRAWN

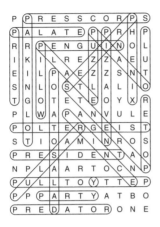

34-35

P
Famous Singers

(ELVIS) PRESLEY
PAUL SIMON
(DOLLY) PARTON
PAT BOONE

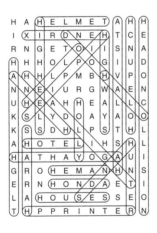

36-37

H
Worn Above the Waist

HAIRNET
HOMBURG
HEADPHONES

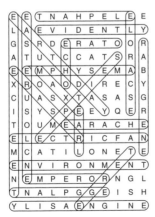

38-39

E
Found in a Classroom

EDUCATOR
ESSAY
EQUATION
ENGLISH

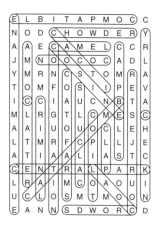

40-41

C
Computer Lingo

CODE
CD-ROM
COMMAND

42-43

W
U.S. Cities

WALLA WALLA
WAUKEGAN
WHEELING

44-45

M
Animals

MOOSE
MUSK OX
MONKEY
MONGOOSE
MINK

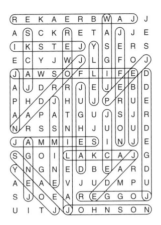

46-47

J
Articles of Clothing

JACKET
JERSEY
JODHPURS
JOG BRA
JUMPSUIT

48-49

K & Y
Vehicles

KNOCKABOUT
KETCH
YAWL
YACHT
YAMAHA MOTORCYCLE

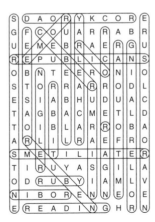

50-51

R
Foreign Cities

RABAT
RIYADH

52-53

S
Things in the Sky

SATURN
SUPERMAN
SNOWFLAKES

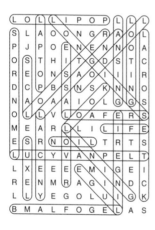

54-55

L
Fictional Characters

LONG JOHN SILVER
(THE) LITTLE MERMAID
LEGOLAS

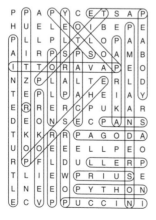

56-57

P
Composers

PACHELBEL
(COLE) PORTER
PURCELL
POULENC

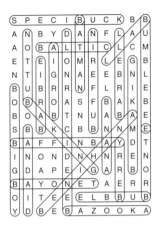

58-59

B
Notorious People

BABY FACE NELSON
BONAPARTE

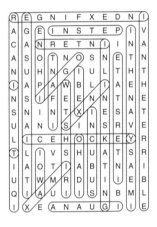

60-61

I
Found in a Hospital

INSULIN
IV TUBE

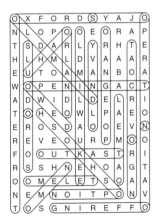

62-63

O
Things You Wear

OPERA HAT
OBI
OVERSHOES

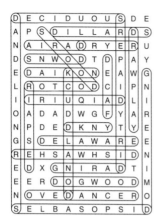

64-65

D
Cartoon Characters

DEPUTY DAWG
DEXTER

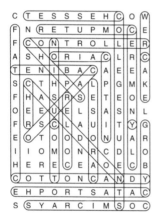

66-67

C
Things in Outer Space

CONSTELLATION
CERES

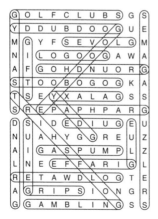

68-69

G
Holiday Things

GUY FAWKES DAY
GREETINGS

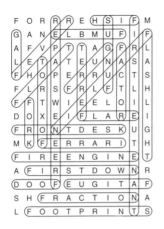

70-71

F
Titles People Have

FOREMAN
FATHER
FIELD MARSHAL

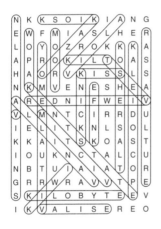

72-73

K & V
Birds

KINGFISHER
KESTREL
KOOKABURRA
VIREO

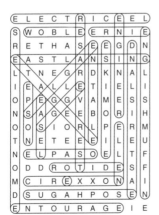

74-75

E
Boys' Names

ETHAN
ELIOT
EDDIE

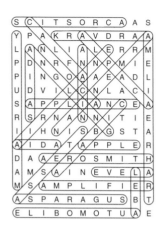

76-77

A
Medicine/Drugs

ASPIRIN
ADVIL
ANTIHISTAMINE

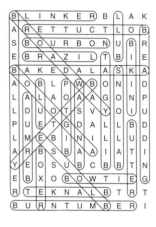

78-79

B
Desserts

BAKLAVA
BISCOTTI

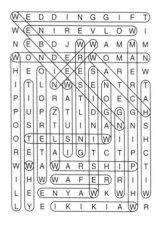

80-81

W
Vehicles

WINDJAMMER
WRECKER

141

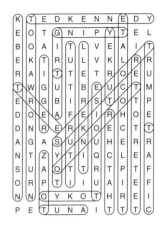

82-83

T
Foreign Cities

TEL AVIV
TAIPEI

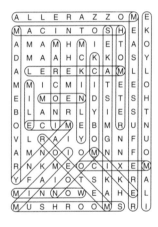

84-85

M
Fish

MAHI-MAHI
MARLIN
MONKFISH

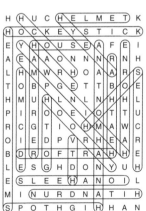

86-87

H
Fictional Characters

HUCK FINN
HOT LIPS HOULIHAN

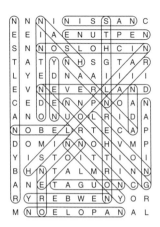

88-89

N
Personality Traits

NICE
NASTY
NAIVE
NONCOMMITTAL
NORMAL

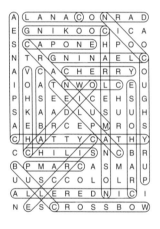

90-91

C
Authors

(TRUMAN) CAPOTE
(GEOFFREY) CHAUCER
(ALBERT) CAMUS
(JACKIE) COLLINS

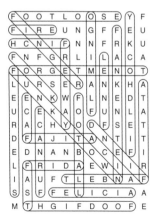

92-93

F
Songs

FUN, FUN, FUN
FLASHDANCE
FAME

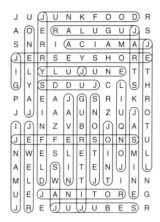

94-95

J
Movie Titles

JURASSIC PARK
(THE) JAZZ SINGER

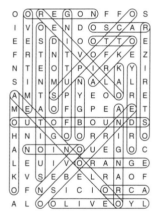

96-97

O
Football Terms

OFFSIDE
OFFENSE
OPEN RECEIVER
OFFICIAL

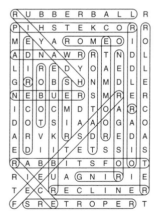

98-99

R
Famous Singers

RAY DAVIES
(BONNIE) RAITT

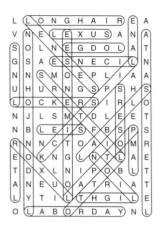

100-101

L
Things From the Sixties

LAVA LAMP
LAUGH-IN
LSD
(JOHN) LENNON
LIBERATION

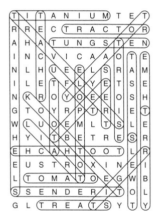

102-103

T
Words Ending in "LY"

TECHNICALLY
TRULY
TRUSTINGLY

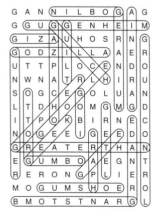

104-105

G
Things in the Wild West

GANG
GHOST TOWN
GOLD MINE
GERONIMO

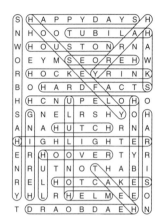

106-107

H
TV Shows

(THE) HONEYMOONERS
HART TO HART

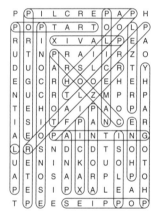

108-109

P
Names of People in the Bible

PHARAOH
PONTIUS PILATE

110-111

I
Money Lingo

INTEREST
INFLATION
INSIDER TRADING

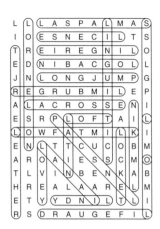

112-113

L
College Majors

LITERATURE
LIBERAL ARTS

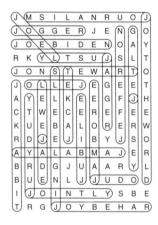

114-115

J
Foods

JERKY
JARLSBERG

116-117

A
Colleges/Universities

ALABAMA
ANTIOCH
ADELPHI

118-119

K & U
Things With Tails

KOMODO DRAGON
KANGAROO
KITE
UNDERDOG

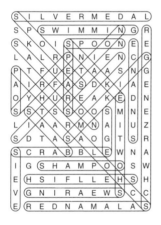

120-121

S
Kitchen Utensils

SKILLET
SALAD TONGS

122-123

N
Notorious People

NAPOLEON
NORMAN BATES

124-125

E
Girls' Names

ELIZABETH
EMILY
ELAINE

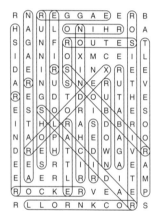

126-127

R
Famous Women

REBA MCENTIRE
(JOAN) RIVERS

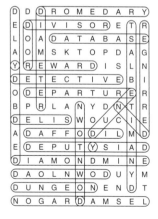

128-129

D
Computer Lingo

DESKTOP
DISPLAY
DOCUMENT

Pages 10-11   T
1 THOMAS, TERRY
2 TUSCALOOSA, TALLAHASSEE
3 TEMPERATURE, TUNDRA
4 TEXTBOOKS, TAPE
5 TIMBERWOLVES, TITANS
6 TERMITE, TICK
7 TOAST, TRIX
8 TABLE, TEA CART
9 TODAY, TELETUBBIES
10 TENTACLES, TITANIC
11 TAFT, TYLER
12 TRIDENT, TRISCUITS

Pages 30-31   B
1 BANANA, BEETS
2 BLUES BROTHERS, BEE GEES
3 BILLS, BOX OF STATIONERY
4 BAHAMAS, BERMUDA
5 BERIBERI, BOTULISM
6 BANK, BIG BUCKS
7 BABY RUTH, BOTTLES
8 BATMAN, BEN-HUR
9 BINGO, BOGGLE
10 BRACELET, BELT
11 BUDWEISER, BECKS
12 BALLOONS, BAREBACK RIDER

Pages 50-51   R
1 ROAST BEEF, REUBEN
2 RETAIL ITEMS, RUGS
3 REPUBLICANS, REAGAN
4 READING, RELIGION
5 RAN OUT OF TIME, ROAD
  CLOSURE
6 ROCKY ROAD, RUM RAISIN
7 RABBIT, RUBBER BALL
8 RACHAEL RAY, RAVEN
9 ROLLERBLADING, ROBIN
10 ROME, RIO
11 RUBY, ROSETTA STONE
12 RECORDER, REBEC

Pages 70-71   F
1 FERRET, FISH
2 FIRE ENGINE, FERRARI
3 FOX TROT, FRUG
4 FOOD, FORK
5 FUMBLE, FIRST DOWN
6 FOOTPRINTS, FUNGUS
7 FRONT DESK, FREE
  NEWSPAPER
8 FRACTION, FACTOR
9 FLASHLIGHT, FLARE
10 FLAG, FLOAT
11 FATIGUE, FEVER
12 FRAULEIN, FIRST
  LIEUTENANT

Pages 90-91   C
1 CRAB HOUSE, CHILI'S
2 (AL) CAPONE, CHARLES
  MANSON
3 CASABA, CHERRY
4 COUGH SYRUP, CAPLET
5 CHATTY CATHY, CRANIUM
6 CLEANING, COOKING
7 CASPIAN SEA, CANAL
8 (ANTON) CHEKHOV,
  (JOSEPH) CONRAD
9 CINDERELLA, CLOWN
10 CROSSBOW, CLUB
11 COIN, CIRCLE
12 CARDIO, CRAMP

Pages 110-111   I
1 INCOME, INVESTMENT
2 ICE CREAM, ITALIAN ICE
3 IGNITION, INSTRUMENT
  PANEL
4 IRAQ, IRAN
5 ISLANDER, IVAN LENDL
6 IBUPROFEN, IODINE
7 IGLOO, INUIT
8 ITUNES, IMPORT
9 IRENE, INGRID
10 INNING, INFIELD
11 INDIGO, IVORY
12 I SPY, I LOVE LUCY

Pages 12-13   F
1 FRIDA KAHLO, (BETTY) FRIEDAN
2 FLU MEDICINE, FLONASE
3 FENCE, FILING CABINET
4 FISHING, FOOTBALL
5 FIREMAN, FIRST LIEUTENANT
6 FANS, FAX MACHINE
7 FERRET, FLEA
8 FRENCH, FARSI
9 FATHER, FELIX
10 FRIES, FUDGE
11 FLOWER, FRIENDSHIPS
12 FORD, FOOT LOCKER

Pages 32-33   W
1 WATERCRESS, WAX BEAN
2 WYOMING, WELFARE
3 WASTE, WEEDS
4 WARDEN, WET NURSE
5 WESTINGHOUSE, WASHER
6 WILE E. COYOTE, WALDO
7 WHISKEY, WINE
8 WINGS, WU-TANG CLAN
9 WAL-MART, WENDY'S
10 WATERBOY, WIDE RECEIVER
11 WALNUT, WILLOW
12 WARY, WOODEN

Pages 52-53   S
1 SATCHMO, SHAQ
2 STARS, SATELLITE
3 SAUCE, SAUSAGE
4 STANFORD, SMITH
5 SALMON, SARDINE
6 SAUDI ARABIA, SRI LANKA
7 SNOW LEOPARD, SKIN
8 SHAKESPEARE, STALIN
9 STRANGERS, SOLITUDE
10 SQUARE MILE, SECONDS
11 SHELVES, SOFA
12 (THE) SCARLET LETTER, (THE) STAND

Pages 72-73   K & V
1 KIWI, VULTURE
2 KNIFE, VICTIM
3 KILOBYTE, VIRTUAL MEMORY
4 KA-POW!, VROOM!
5 KILT, VEST
6 KNICKS, VIKINGS
7 KAZOO, VIOLA
8 KOSHER SALT, VANILLA
9 KIOSK, VALISE
10 KENT STATE, VASSAR
11 KALEIDOSCOPE, VIEWFINDER
12 KISS, VAN HALEN

Pages 92-93   F
1 FOOTBALL, FIELD HOCKEY
2 FOOTLOOSE, FUNKYTOWN
3 FACE, FINGER
4 FAJITA, FRITTATA
5 FIRE, FOOD FIGHT
6 FLAMINGO, FINCH
7 FELICIA, FRIDA
8 FREEWAY, FAST
9 FORK, FUNNEL
10 FRANKENSTEIN, FIEND
11 FORGET-ME-NOT, FLEUR-DE-LIS
12 FURNACE, FAN BELT

Pages 112-113   L
1 LORD NELSON, LIFEGUARD
2 LINGERIE, LOCKET
3 LOVEY, LAMBKIN
4 LIMBO, LINDY
5 LENS CAP, LEATHER
6 LEAR JET, LIMO
7 LANAI, LAS PALMAS
8 LATIN, LINGUISTICS
9 LOW-FAT MILK, LIMBURGER
10 LOG CABIN, LOFT
11 LIP GLOSS, LICENSE
12 LACROSSE, LONG JUMP

Pages 14-15   S
1 SKIRT, SOCKS
2 SHERBET, SHORTCAKE
3 SEAT BELT, SUSPENSION
4 SASKATCHEWAN, SERBIA
5 SAM SNEAD, SURFER
6 SINK, SAYS
7 SODA, SPINACH
8 SHEEP, SWINE
9 SEVENTH, SOUTH
10 SANDCASTLE, SUNBLOCK
11 SEPIA, SILVER
12 SCREWDRIVER,
   SNOW SHOVEL

Pages 34-35   P
1 PLATE, POTATO SALAD
2 PILLOW, PALATE
3 POLTERGEIST, PREDATOR
4 PRESIDENT, PRESS CORPS
5 PULL TOY, PUZZLE
6 PRIEST, PARENTS
7 PHOENIX, PIZZA OVEN
8 PLUTO, PULSAR
9 POSTER, PARTY
10 PENGUIN, PIANO
11 PRINCE, (TOM) PETTY
12 PRIZES, PARKING LOT

Pages 54-55   L
1 LUCY VAN PELT, LASSIE
2 LASAGNA, LEG OF LAMB
3 LIFE, LOOK
4 LONDON, LANSING
5 LOLLIPOP, LEMON DROPS
6 LAPTOP, LEXUS
7 LOAFERS, LACES
8 LONGINGS, LOVER
9 LINGERIE, LINING
10 LION, LOBSTER
11 LACROSSE STICK, LUGE
12 LARCENY, LOOTING

Pages 74-75   E
1 ERNIE, ERIC
2 EAST LANSING, EL PASO
3 EVEREST, ESKIMO PIE
4 EASEL, ERASER
5 EDMONTON OILERS, EAGLES
6 ENGINEER, EDITOR
7 EGGS, ENGLISH MUFFIN
8 ETAGERE, END TABLE
9 ENTOURAGE, ELLEN
10 ELECTRIC EEL,
   EASTER ISLAND
11 ELBOW, ESOPHAGUS
12 EPSON, EXXON

Pages 94-95   J
1 JUNE, JULY
2 (THE) JUDDS, JETHRO TULL
3 JAVELIN, JARTS
4 JAMAICA,
   (THE) JERSEY SHORE
5 JAY LENO, JERRY SEINFELD
6 JITTERBUG, JIG
7 JUNK FOOD, JUJUBES
8 JAWS, JUMANJI
9 JONQUIL, JASMINE
10 JUGULAR, JOINT
11 JEFFERSONS, JETSONS
12 JANITOR, JEWELER

Pages 114-115   J
1 JELL-O, JAMBALAYA
2 JACKET, JERSEY
3 (THOMAS) JEFFERSON,
   JOE BIDEN
4 JOURNALISM, JUDO
5 JET LAG, JURY DUTY
6 JOY TO THE WORLD,
   JINGLE BELLS
7 JACKRABBIT, JOGGER
8 JON STEWART, JOY BEHAR
9 JUSTLY, JOINTLY
10 JUBILEE, JAMBOREE
11 JADE, JEWEL
12 (BILLY) JOEL, (MICK) JAGGER

Pages 16-17 I
1 (THE) INCREDIBLES,
   IVANHOE
2 IRISH LINEN, IVORY
3 I LOVE YOU, I'M YOURS
4 ILLUSTRATOR, INTERN
5 IRON, IODINE
6 INDY CAR, IMPALA
7 ISLE, INDONESIA
8 INTERIOR DESIGN, ITALIAN
9 ICE CREAM, ICE MILK
10 (BILLY) IDOL,
   (ENRIQUE or JULIO) IGLESIAS
11 ID CARD, IBUPROFEN
12 ICARUS, ISIS

Pages 36-37 H
1 HELMET, HOOD
2 HEADLIGHT, HALO
3 HOUSES, HIGHWAYS
4 HE-MAN, HATHA YOGA
5 HUNTER, HYENA
6 HELLO, HASTA LA VISTA
7 HIPPIES, (JIMI) HENDRIX
8 HOLLY, HANUKKAH GELT
9 HOLE PUNCH, HP PRINTER
10 HANDS, HIGH HEELS
11 HEAD-ON COLLISION,
   HONDA
12 HOTEL, HARRAH'S

Pages 56-57 P
1 POST-IT, PASTE
2 PULITZER, PEABODY
3 PORSCHE, PRIUS
4 PARSLEY, PAPRIKA
5 PROKOFIEV, PUCCINI
6 POWDER, PRELL
7 PAVAROTTI, PAMELA
   ANDERSON
8 PANS, PEELER
9 PYTHON, PAINTED TURTLE
10 PALACE, PAGODA
11 POKER, POLO
12 POLLEN, PETS

Pages 76-77 A
1 AMELIA EARHART, AIDA
2 ANACIN, ALEVE
3 AIRPLANE, AUTOMOBILE
4 ACROSTICS, ANGLING
5 AEROSMITH, AIR SUPPLY
6 APPLIANCE, AMPLIFIER
7 AARDVARK, ALPACA
8 ARABIC, ARMENIAN
9 ADAM, ABEL
10 APPLE, ASPARAGUS
11 ACORN, ASSETS
12 ADIDAS, AFLAC

Pages 96-97 O
1 ONION, OKRA
2 OREGON, OKLAHOMA
3 OCTOPUS, ORCA
4 OB/GYN, ORDERLY
5 OSTERIZER, OVEN
6 OLIVE OYL,
   OTTO (on "The Simpsons")
7 OOLONG TEA, ORANGINA
8 (DONNY) OSMOND,
   (OZZY) OSBOURNE
9 OSCAR, OLIVIER
10 OUT OF BOUNDS, OVERTIME
11 ORANGE, OAK
12 OSTENTATIOUS,
   OFF-PUTTING

Pages 116-117 A
1 ANNIE, ALEX
2 AIRPLANE, ARIES
3 ARTICHOKE, ASPARAGUS
4 AMHERST, AUBURN
5 ANCHOVY, ALBACORE
6 ANGOLA, ALBANIA
7 ACNE SUFFERER, APPALOOSA
8 ADAMS, ARCHIMEDES
9 AGING, AVALANCHE
10 AREA, ACRE
11 ARMCHAIR, ASHTRAY
12 ANIMAL FARM,
   ANNA KARENINA

Pages 18-19 M
1 MEATLOAF, MONTE CRISTO
2 MERCHANDISE, MITTENS
3 MARCOS, MEIR
4 MATH, MUSIC
5 MISSED THE BUS, MIGRAINE
6 MINT, MOCHA
7 MAKEUP, MASCARA
8 MILEY CYRUS,
   (PENNY) MARSHALL
9 MOUNTAIN, MOSS
10 MECCA, MILAN
11 MALACHITE, MOONSTONE
12 MANDOLIN, MARACAS

Pages 38-39 E
1 ELEPHANT, ENCLOSURE
2 ENGINE, ELECTRIC FAN
3 EAGLE, EGRET
4 EGGPLANT, ESCAROLE
5 EVIDENTLY, EASILY
6 ENVIRONMENT, ENERGY BAR
7 ERATO, ECHO
8 EASTER, EARTH DAY
9 ERASER, EXAM
10 EXCITEMENT, EMPTIES
11 EARACHE, EMPHYSEMA
12 EARL, EMPEROR

Pages 58-59 B
1 BOB'S BIG BOY, BENIHANA
2 BENEDICT ARNOLD, BORGIA
3 BANANA, BERRY
4 BUFFERIN, BAND-AID
5 BALL, BARBIE
6 BAKING, BEDMAKING
7 BALTIC, BAFFIN BAY
8 (PEARL) BUCK, BRONTË
9 BATMAN, BUMBLEBEE
10 BAYONET, BAZOOKA
11 BUTTON, BUBBLE
12 BICEPS, BARBELL

Pages 78-79 B
1 BLOUSE, BOW TIE
2 BREAD PUDDING,
   BAKED ALASKA
3 BATTERY, BLINKER
4 BRAZIL, BERMUDA
5 BASEBALL PLAYER, BOXER
6 BIG TOP, BALLOONS
7 BUTTER, BOLOGNA
8 BULL, BILLY GOAT
9 BROADWAY, BOURBON
10 BLANKET, BIKINI
11 BLUE, BURNT UMBER
12 BAND SAW, BOLT CUTTER

Pages 98-99 R
1 RADIO, RECORD
2 RABBIT'S FOOT, RECLINER
3 ROCKET SHIP, ROBOT
4 ROSE GARDEN, REPORTERS
5 RUBBER BALL, RUBIK'S CUBE
6 RING, RICE
7 RIYADH, RWANDA
8 ROMEO, (THE) RIDDLER
9 READING LAMP, ROOMMATE
10 REUBEN, ROAST BEEF
11 (LINDA) RONSTADT,
   (LEANN) RIMES
12 RIDE, ROLLER COASTER

Pages 118-119 K & U
1 KING KONG, ULYSSES
2 KNISH, UPSIDE-DOWN CAKE
3 KILT, UNDIES
4 KABUL, ULAN BATOR
5 KIT KAT, UNWRAPPED
6 KMART, U-HAUL
7 KEDS, UGGS
8 KATE WINSLET,
   UMA THURMAN
9 KENTUCKY, UTAH
10 KOALA, UNICORN
11 KAYAK, UNEVEN BARS
12 KILLING, USURY

Pages 20-21   O
 1 OLLIE, OZZY
 2 ORION, OSPREY
 3 ONION, OREGANO
 4 OHIO STATE, OBERLIN
 5 OCTOPUS, ORANGE ROUGHY
 6 OMAN,
   OCEANIA (from Orwell's "1984")
 7 OCELOT, ORANGUTAN
 8 ORVILLE WRIGHT,
   (ANNIE) OAKLEY
 9 OPEN SEA, ORAL SURGERY
10 OUNCE, OHM
11 OUTLET, OXYGEN
12 OLIVER TWIST,
   ON THE ROAD

Pages 40-41   C
 1 CACTI, CAMEL
 2 CLUE, CRIMINAL
 3 CONFIGURATION,
   COMPATIBLE
 4 CLAP, CLATTER
 5 CHOWDER, CAMPBELL'S
 6 COSINE, CALCULUS
 7 CATACOMB, COAL
 8 CALAMITY JANE, CAVALRY
 9 CHECK-IN, COPILOT
10 COCOON, COMMA
11 CENTRAL PARK, CROWDS
12 COURT JESTER,
   COAT OF ARMS

Pages 60-61   I
 1 ICE HOCKEY,
   INLINE SKATING
 2 IN THE NAVY, I'M EASY
 3 INSTEP, INDEX FINGER
 4 ITALIAN SAUSAGE,
   IRISH STEW
 5 INSULT, "I QUIT!"
 6 IGUANA, IBEX
 7 IOWA, IDAHO
 8 INXS, INCUBUS
 9 IN A CAR, INTERSTATE
10 IAGO, IVAN THE TERRIBLE
11 IPHONE, IMAX
12 INTERN, INFANT

Pages 80-81   W
 1 WONDER WOMAN,
   WOLVERINE
 2 WEDDING GIFT, WATCH
 3 WREN, WHIPPOORWILL
 4 WALTZ, WATUSI
 5 WETSUIT, WITCH'S HAT
 6 WAGON, WARSHIP
 7 WAIKIKI, WEST INDIES
 8 WRITING, WEB DESIGN
 9 WHIPPING CREAM, WHEY
10 WINE, WAFER
11 (JOHN) WAYNE,
   (KATE) WINSLET
12 WRESTLING, WATER POLO

Pages 100-101   L
 1 LIPSTICK, LEIS
 2 LIGHT, LAMP
 3 LICENSE, LOTTO
 4 LOCKERS, LIFTERS
 5 LION, LODGE
 6 LATER, LONG TIME NO SEE
 7 LONG HAIR,
   LYNDON B. JOHNSON
 8 LETTERS TO SANTA,
   LABOR DAY
 9 LAPTOP, LABELS
10 LENSES, LUNGS
11 LEXUS, LANE
12 LUXOR, LOSERS

Pages 120-121   S
 1 SITUATION, SYRUP
 2 SCHOLARSHIP,
   SILVER MEDAL
 3 SEDAN, SAAB
 4 SAGE, SAFFRON
 5 SMOKING, SWEARING
 6 SOAP, SHAMPOO
 7 (ARNOLD)
   SCHWARZENEGGER,
   (BRITNEY) SPEARS
 8 SPOON, SIEVE
 9 SNAKE, SALAMANDER
10 SHOWTIME, SUNDANCE
11 SWIMMING, SCRABBLE
12 SHELLFISH, SPORES

Pages 22-23 D
1 DILBERT, DWARF
2 DECAF, DESSERTS
3 DISCOVER, DETAILS
4 DENVER, DAKAR
5 DUBBLE BUBBLE, DROPS
6 DIAMOND RING, DIGITAL CAMERA
7 DANCE SHOE, DOCKSIDER
8 DIARY, DARK SECRET
9 DRESS, DRAWERS
10 DEER, DUCK
11 DRIVER, DISCUS
12 DRUG DEALING, DEFRAUDING

Pages 42-43 W
1 WAYNE, WESLEY
2 WICHITA, WACO
3 WINDSTORM, WINTER
4 WORKSHEET, WITE-OUT
5 WHITE SOX, WIZARDS
6 WASP, WEEVIL
7 WAFFLE, WHEATIES
8 WICKER CHAIR, WALL UNIT
9 (THE) WALTONS, (THE) WEST WING
10 WHALE, WALRUS
11 WASHINGTON, WILSON
12 WITNESS, WRIT

Pages 62-63 O
1 OATMEAL, OMELET
2 OUTKAST, (THE) O'JAYS
3 OSHKOSH, OLD NAVY
4 ORLANDO, OAHU
5 ORGAN, OFFERING
6 OPTION, OWED
7 ORANGE POP, OREOS
8 ON THE WATERFRONT, (THE) OMEN
9 OPERATION, OLD MAID
10 OXFORDS, OVERCOAT
11 O'DOULS, OLD MILWAUKEE
12 OPENING ACT, OVATION

Pages 82-83 T
1 TURKEY, TUNA
2 TOYS, TROUSERS
3 TED KENNEDY, (MARGARET) THATCHER
4 TRIG, TYPING
5 TOOK A WRONG TURN, TRAFFIC
6 TUTTI-FRUTTI, TRIPLE CHOCOLATE
7 TINKERBELL, TIGGER
8 TED DANSON, (ALEX) TREBEK
9 TREE, TEETER-TOTTER
10 TOKYO, TORONTO
11 TURQUOISE, TOPAZ
12 TRUMPET, TUBA

Pages 102-103 T
1 TIGER, TORTOISE
2 TOYOTA, TRACTOR
3 TEPEE, TOTEM POLE
4 TUNGSTEN, TITANIUM
5 TOTALLY, TERRIBLY
6 TRAIL, TREES
7 TOWELS, TRAVELERS
8 TOFU, TOMATO
9 TEACHER, TEXTBOOK
10 THEME, TREATS
11 TIREDNESS, TOOTHACHE
12 TRAINING WHEELS, TASSELS

Pages 122-123 N
1 NIKE, NESTLÉ
2 NERO, NAZIS
3 NECTARINE, NAVEL ORANGE
4 NOSE SPRAY, NODOZ
5 NERF BALL, NINTENDO
6 NEATENING UP, NEEDLEWORK
7 NILE, NORTH SEA
8 NABOKOV, NOVELIST
9 NINJA, NURSE
10 NUNCHAKU, NUCLEAR
11 NICKEL, NEST
12 "NO PAIN, NO GAIN," NAUTILUS MACHINE

Pages 24-25   G
1 GLUE, GREASE
2 GRAMMY, GRADUATION
3 GREMLIN, GAS GUZZLER
4 GINGER, GINSENG
5 GAMBLING, GOOFING OFF
6 GILLETTE RAZOR, GLEEM
7 GARBO, GENE SIMMONS
8 GARLIC PRESS, GRATER
9 GATOR, GECKO
10 GRAND CANYON, GEYSER
11 GOLF, GARDENING
12 GRASS, GLUTEN

Pages 44-45   M
1 MADONNA, MARIE CURIE
2 METHADONE, MAALOX
3 MOTOR, MOBILE
4 MOVIES, MACRAME
5 MAIL CARRIER, MIDSHIPMAN
6 MODEM, MIXER
7 MOLE, MOBY DICK
8 MANDARIN, MONGOLIAN
9 MARY, MICAH
10 M&MS, MILK DUDS
11 MARIGOLD, MAGNOLIA
12 MICROSOFT, METLIFE

Pages 64-65   D
1 DAIKON,
   DANDELION GREENS
2 DELAWARE, DESPAIR
3 DIRTY DIAPERS,
   DISPOSABLES
4 DOCTOR, DANCER
5 DRYER, DISHWASHER
6 DONALD DUCK, DARIA
7 DAIQUIRI, DECAF
8 DEVO, (THE) DOORS
9 DKNY, DILLARD'S
10 DOWNS, DRAW PLAY
11 DOGWOOD, DECIDUOUS
12 DOMINEERING, DARING

Pages 84-85   M
1 MIKE, MANNY
2 MOON, METEOR
3 MUSHROOMS, MOZZARELLA
4 MOUNT HOLYOKE, MIAMI
5 MACKEREL, MINNOW
6 MEXICO, MALI
7 MEASLES SUFFERER, MOTH
8 MARCONI, MCKINLEY
9 MICE, MAKING MISTAKES
10 MILE, METER
11 MACINTOSH, MOEN
12 MADAME BOVARY,
   MOBY-DICK

Pages 104-105   G
1 GOBI, GIZA
2 GUILT, GUMSHOE
3 GOOGLE, GEEK
4 GRENADE, GODZILLA
5 GAZPACHO, GUMBO
6 GREATER THAN, GRAPH
7 GROTTO, GOPHER
8 GULCH, GUNSLINGER
9 GATE, GROUND CONTROL
10 GERANIUM, GARDENIA
11 (THE) GUGGENHEIM,
   GRANT'S TOMB
12 GRETEL, GOBLIN

Pages 124-125   E
1 EQUESTRIAN, EPEE
2 ENDLESS LOVE, ESO BESO
3 EYELID, EARLOBE
4 EMPANADA, EGG ROLL
5 EUREKA!, EGAD!
6 EAGLE, EGRET
7 EDIE, ERICA
8 EXPRESSWAY, ELEVATOR
9 EGG TIMER,
   ESPRESSO MAKER
10 EXAMPLE, EVIL EYE
11 EASTER LILY, EDELWEISS
12 ENGINE, ERRATA

Pages 26-27 A
1 ASIAN, ARBY'S
2 ATTILA THE HUN,
   AL CAPONE
3 APPLE, APRICOT
4 ASPIRIN, ADVIL
5 ACTION FIGURE, AEROBIE
6 ADD AIR TO TIRES,
   ARRANGE FILES
7 ATLANTIC (OCEAN),
   AMAZON (RIVER)
8 (JANE) AUSTEN,
   (ISAAC) ASIMOV
9 ANGEL, ANIMAL
10 ARMS, ARROW
11 ARCHERY TARGET, ASHTRAY
12 AEROBIC, ACHE

Pages 46-47 J
1 JEANS, JAMMIES
2 JAWBREAKER, JUJUBE
3 JENGA, JACKS
4 JAPAN, JORDAN
5 JOGGER, JAVELIN THROWER
6 JUGHEAD, JUDGE DREDD
7 JUICE, JELLY
8 JACKAL, JOEY
9 JEFFERSON, JOHNSON
10 JET SKI, JEEP
11 JADE, JASMINE
12 JIGSAW, JAWS OF LIFE

Pages 66-67 C
1 CHIPS, COOLER
2 CUSHION, CLAY
3 CYBORG, CATASTROPHE
4 CABINET, CHIEF OF STAFF
5 CHESS SET, CONTROLLER
6 CAKE, CEREMONY
7 CAIRO, CAULDRON
8 COMET, COSMIC RAYS
9 COLLEGE STUDENTS,
   COMPUTER
10 CAPTAIN, CREW
11 CARUSO, CHER
12 CAROUSEL, COTTON CANDY

Pages 86-87 H
1 HANNAH MONTANA,
   HERCULES
2 HAMBURGER, HOT DOG
3 HOORAY!, HELP ME!
4 HARTFORD, HANOI
5 HO HOS, HEATH BAR
6 HOUSE, HDTV
7 HEELS, HIGH-TOPS
8 HOOCH, HEALTH PROBLEMS
9 HEMINGWAY, HAWTHORNE
10 HYENA, HARE
11 HOCKEY STICK, HELMET
12 HIT-AND-RUN, HOMICIDE

Pages 106-107 H
1 HARRY, HENRY
2 HOUSTON, HONOLULU
3 HOCKEY RINK, HARD FACTS
4 HIGHLIGHTER, HOLE PUNCH
5 HAWKS, HEAT
6 HOUSEFLY, HONEYBEE
7 HOTCAKES, HASH BROWNS
8 HEADBOARD, HUTCH
9 HEROES, HAPPY DAYS
10 HALIBUT, HERRING
11 HOOVER, HARRISON
12 HULL, HELM

Pages 126-127 R
1 RATTLE, ROCKER
2 ROSIE THE RIVETER
   (BETSY or DIANA) ROSS
3 ROUTES, ROLODEX
4 RUNNING SHOES, RUBDOWN
5 RIFLE, RHINO
6 RADISH, RUTABAGA
7 RADICALS, RICHARD NIXON
8 REINDEER, RUDOLPH
9 REAGAN, ROOSEVELT
10 RIBBONS, RIDES
11 REST AREA, RAMP
12 ROCK 'N' ROLL, REGGAE

Pages 28-29 N
1 NASCAR, NINEPINS
2 NAME GAME,
   NOWHERE MAN
3 NECK, NOSTRIL
4 NACHOS, NAAN
5 NEVER!, NEXT!
6 NIGHTINGALE, NUTHATCH
7 NANCY, NAOMI
8 NEW YORK, NORTH DAKOTA
9 NUTCRACKER, NAPKINS
10 NURSE RATCHED, NESSIE
11 NARCISSUS, NASTURTIUM
12 NEON, NITROGEN

Pages 48-49 K & Y
1 KOOL-AID, YOOHOO
2 KWANZAA, YOM KIPPUR
3 KITE, YO-YO
4 KING KONG, YETI
5 KARO SYRUP, YEAST
6 KAYAK, YUGO
7 KAUAI, YUCATAN
8 KENO, YAHTZEE
9 KEFIR, YOGURT
10 KEYCHAIN, YANKEES CAP
11 KATYDID, YELLOWJACKET
12 KOREAN, YIDDISH

Pages 68-69 G
1 GARLAND, GOLF SHIRT
2 GALAXY, GENIUS
3 GAS PUMP, GOOGOL
4 GYMNASTS, GRIPS
5 GIRAFFE, GUIDE
6 G'DAY, GOOD-BYE
7 GOLDWATER, GO-GO BOOTS
8 GIFTS, GROUNDHOG
9 GLUE, GRAPH PAPER
10 GLOVES, GOLF CLUBS
11 GAS GUZZLERS,
   GOOD BUDDY
12 GAMBLING, GAMES

Pages 88-89 N
1 NESTLÉ CANDY BAR,
   NOUGAT
2 NOBEL, NEWBERY
3 NISSAN, NASH
4 NORTHERN LIGHTS,
   NEPTUNE
5 NEUROTIC, NEEDY
6 NAIL POLISH, NAIR
7 (JACK) NICHOLSON,
   (LEONARD) NIMOY
8 NOTHING, NADA
9 NAPOLEON, NERO
10 NARNIA, NEVERLAND
11 NAPPING, NINTENDO
12 NOVEL, NOTE

Pages 108-109 P
1 PANDORA, (NANCY) PELOSI
2 PROZAC, PLAVIX
3 PAPER CLIP, PICKAX
4 PHOTOGRAPHY, PAINTING
5 POLICEMAN, PILOT
6 PHONE, PERCOLATOR
7 PANDA, PARROT
8 POLISH, PORTUGUESE
9 PETER, PAUL
10 POP-TART, PRETZEL
11 PINOCCHIO'S NOSE, POPPIES
12 PRUDENTIAL, PFIZER

Pages 128-129 D
1 DUNE, DROMEDARY
2 DETECTIVE, DEAD BODY
3 DOWNLOAD, DATABASE
4 DYNAMITE BLAST, DIN
5 DOOR, DRAWER
6 DIVISOR, DIAMETER
7 DUNGEON, DIAMOND MINE
8 DEPUTY, DERRINGER
9 DEPARTURE, DELAY
10 DAISY, DAFFODIL
11 DOWNTOWN, DELIS
12 DRAGON, DAMSEL

ABOUT THE AUTHOR

MARK DANNA is one of the most prolific word search puzzle-makers in North America. Author of 15 word search books for Puzzlewright Press and creator of word search puzzles for magazines and corporate clients, Danna has designed more than 1,000 such puzzles—many with playful grid shapes relating to the puzzle's theme. A big fan of Hasbro's *Scattergories*, Danna knows games well: he play-tested hundreds of board and electronic games during a seven-year stint at *Games* magazine, where he also learned the ropes of puzzlemaking from Will Shortz and other top puzzle professionals.

Since 1991, Danna has written United Media's syndicated newspaper puzzle "Wordy Gurdy." He is coauthor of "365 Brain Puzzlers," American Mensa's long-running, annual, page-a-day puzzle calendar. Danna is a regular contributor of various word puzzles to Publications International's *Brain Games* series, and his crosswords have appeared in *The New York Times*.

Danna has also been employed as a staff writer for *Who Wants to Be a Millionaire*, a sports director on Caribbean cruise ships, and a professional Frisbee player. Danna won three national Frisbee titles and cowrote *Frisbee Players' Handbook*, a how-to book that came packaged inside a Wham-O Frisbee disc.